YHS

Busine:

NVQ Level

Business Administration

NVQ Level 1

Lynda Bourne and
Pamela Scott

PITMAN
PUBLISHING

PITMAN PUBLISHING
128 Long Acre, London WC2E 9AN

A Division of Longman Group UK Limited

First published in Great Britain 1993

British Library Cataloguing in Publication Data
A CIP catalogue record for this book is available on request from the British Library.

ISBN 0-273-03942-3

Typeset by Tek-Art,
Addiscombe, Croydon, Surrey
Printed by Bell and Bain Ltd., Glasgow

CONTENTS

INTRODUCTION

This book has been designed to provide trainers and trainees with a fully comprehensive, easily understandable and logically sequenced text. Each unit has been written in accordance with the performance criteria, range statements and underpinning knowledge required by awarding bodies such as RSA and LCCI.

Do-it-yourself tasks are included throughout each unit and can be selected to assess a particular skill or provide evidence of understanding for APL (accreditation of prior learning) purposes. Units can be selected and used as discrete, stand-alone modules, or act as part of a complete text as a guide towards a full NVQ in Business Administration Level 1 Award.

Completion of units will build a comprehensive work folder, supported by evidence of practical assessment carried out in the workplace or by simulated assignments. It is important to remember, however, that NVQ assessment is based upon a trainee's demonstration of practical ability over a period of time and cannot, therefore, be proven by written work alone.

Unit and element numbers follow those in the NVQ assessment folder or book provided by the awarding body. DIY tasks have been given a reference number to help trainers and trainees to keep a record of progress. Questions that may be asked by assessors and verifiers have been included throughout. Each unit concludes with information on how to complete the element, to claim competence and gives sample competence transcript statements.

ACKNOWLEDGEMENTS

During the writing of this book we have had the support of company representatives, colleagues and friends. In particular we would like to mention Mr R D Dyer, Environmental Health Department, Poole Borough Council, and Martin Bedford, Customer Services Centre, Royal Mail Letters, Bournemouth.

We would also like to thank Dennis Scott for his endless proof-reading, Sharon and Jayne for typing and printing, and Jerry, Pete, Kris, Carly, Natalie, Leila and Perri for their patience.

Our thanks to the following for providing illustrative material:

APEX; BT; Gestetner Limited; Hewlett-Packard Ltd; GBC (United Kingdom) Ltd; IBM (United Kingdom) Ltd; R B Jackson; Pitney Bowes plc; The Post Office; Rank Xerox (UK) Ltd; Transad Office Furniture Ltd; and Twinlock plc.

Finally, our thanks to Carolyn Lyne at Pitman Publishing for her direction and guidance.

UNIT 1
Filing

Element 1.1
FILE DOCUMENTS AND OPEN NEW FILES WITHIN AN ESTABLISHED FILING SYSTEM

It is very important that you understand the need for effective storage of information. In an office you will be surrounded by many types of information storage, including the office filing cabinets or database program on the computer. In order to retrieve the correct information quickly, it is vital that you understand how each system works. Remember that each office will use the filing system that best suits its needs. Therefore, you must be able to use and understand how each particular system operates in practice.

Different offices will use different types of equipment to store information, depending upon how confidential the information is, or how long it has to be kept for business or legal requirements. There are a number of filing methods and equipment, and various classifications that may be used to simplify and assist quick retrieval of information. If you and the company you work for wish to be seen as organised and efficient, then you cannot afford to operate a filing system that leaves you scrabbling through piles of paperwork or having to admit that you cannot find a client's file!

Large organisations often use a centralised filing system, which means that all departments keep their files in the same place – the Filing Department. The advantage of this is that, because all files are kept in one place, specialist staff can be employed who are experienced in the storage and retrieval of information. It also saves money in terms of only having to purchase filing equipment for one department instead of for many.

Smaller organisations usually employ a departmental filing system – in other words, each department is responsible for its own storage and retrieval of files. This system allows each department to use methods and classifications that best suit the information being stored and instant access to files can be gained. A departmental system is usually smaller and therefore more manageable. It also allows better storage of confidential material, as only departmental staff with authorisation are allowed access.

Whatever classification is used, it is important that all staff in the office understand how the system works. If files and documents are placed in the correct sequence, this will prevent delays when they need to be retrieved again. Remember that both you and the business for which you work will want to be organised and efficient – you will not achieve this if customers are kept waiting on the telephone, or in person, while you attempt to find their file in a disorganised filing cabinet!

▶ *What classifications are there?*

Files are 'classified' – sorted into a logical order so that quick retrieval is possible. There are five main classifications used for filing:

1 Alphabetical

2 Numerical

3 Subject

4 Geographical

5 Chronological

Alphabetical filing

Files are arranged in alphabetical order, usually by surname or perhaps by the name of the organisation. Primary guide cards are used to identify where files beginning with A, B, C, D, and so on, are placed. These cards help you to go straight to the relevant letter instead of working through the alphabet. Secondary guide cards can also be used to break down each section further. Aa–Ag, Ah–Ap and Aq–Az are three examples of secondary guide cards that allow you to find files more quickly.

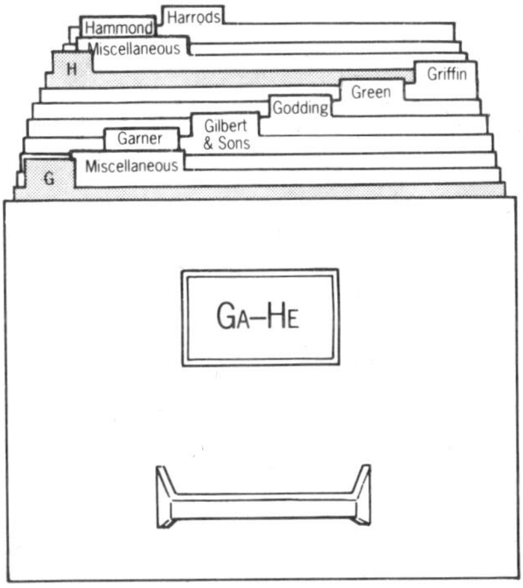

Fig 1.1 An alphabetical filing classification

The advantages of alphabetical filing are:

1 New files are spread throughout the filing cabinets according to the surname or name of the organisation – new files are often used more frequently and this classification prevents congestion in one part of the filing system.

2 You can gain direct access to the files – this means you do not have to use any other classification. You go straight to the filing cabinet and remove the file or document you require.

3 Staff easily recognise the logical sequence of the alphabet – if you are ever in doubt, just look in the telephone directory to see where the name should fit into the alphabetical sequence.

If you do use an alphabetical classification, there are rules that all staff have to follow if files are not to be placed out of sequence. It is essential that you and all other staff are aware of these rules if files are not to be lost!

Rules for alphabetical filing:

1 Use the first letter of the surname or organisation as your primary guide; then the second; third, and so on. For example:

BARBER, J D
BARRY, K
BINNEY, T
BURNS, D F
BYRNE, L

2 If names are the same, order the files according to the initial. If there is no initial, this name comes before a name with one initial – which would come before a name with two initials, and so on. For example:

COLLINS
COLLINS, S
COLLINS, S J
COLLINS, W
COLLINS, W D

3 Ignore titles, although you will still need to record these for correspondence. For example:

DERBY, Miss K L
DEVONSHIRE, Mr F G
DIXON, Sergeant-Major F J
DORSET, Rev B
DULL, Ms M

4 Hyphenated names are filed under the first letter of the first name. For example:

EBONY, L K J
EVANS, L K
EVANS-MOORE, P
EWART, O
EWART-HARRIS, S

5 If names begin with 'Mc', 'McC' or 'Mac' they are all classified as if spelt 'MAC': For example:

McBRIDE, A
McCLOUD, M
MACDONALD, K Y
McKINLEY, Y
MACKINLEY, Y T

6 Names beginning 'St' or 'Saint' are both classified as if spelt 'SAINT'. For example:

ST Peter's College
SAINT Saviour's Rest Home
SAINT Vincent's Food Supplies

7 Ignore 'The', 'A' and 'An' in the name of companies. For example:

The SELECT Food Company Ltd
SEMPLE Associates
SHARPE, K W
A SINGLE Stitch

8 Treat numbers as if they are spelt in full. For example:

FARMER, P L
FERN, D
404 Club
FURNESS, G H

9 Names beginning with a prefix such as 'de', 'du', 'von', 'van', 'O', etc, are treated as part of the main name. You must remember, however, that 'nothing comes before something' – that is why VAN Morrissey comes before VANDY in this example:

O'GRADY, T
O'MALLY, L
VAN MORRISSEY, J
VANDY, Philippa
VON TRAPP & Co

10 District councils, local authorities and boroughs are filed under the name of the district. For example:

BEXLEY, London Borough of
CROYDON, London Borough of
LAMBETH, London Borough of

■ DIY 1.1.1

Copy the following list of names, but rearrange them into correct alphabetical order. (Ignore the figures in brackets.)

(1) JULIE BARLOW	(2) STUART BIGGS	(3) JAMIE DRUMMOND
(4) SARAH NODES	(5) JOHN O'SHEA	(6) ABIGAIL REDDIN
(7) MARC PERRY	(8) JO THOMAS	(9) FAYE JONES
(10) PAUL COCKER	(11) KAREN CHAN	(12) NOREEN AHMED
(13) RUSSELL ELCOCK	(14) TYRONE SHAFIE	(15) RICHARD SIMMS
(16) JEREMY WITTS	(17) ZUBEYR OSKARA	(18) FAYE KAVANAGH
(19) JAMREE ANUKOT	(20) JENNA MACKETT	

Did you remember to do this by surname?

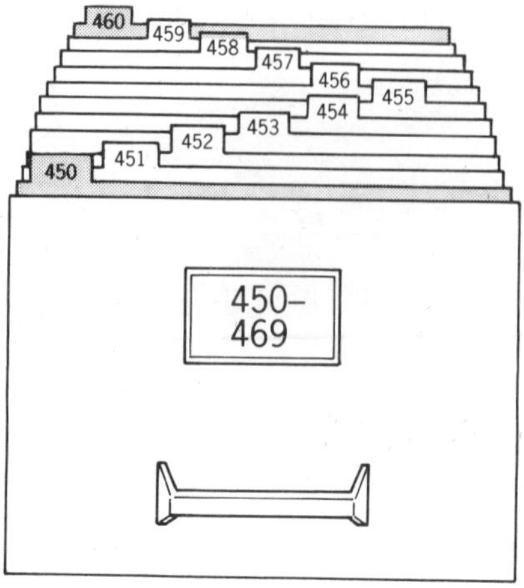

Fig 1.2 A numerical filing classification

Numerical filing

This requires each person or company to have their own personal identity number, like an employee number or customer account number. Each file is placed in numerical order according to this number. Filing by numbers is normally very simple, because there are no set rules to follow, as in alphabetical filing. However, it is important to file in the correct numerical sequence and not to leave out or mix up figures – this would result in files being very difficult to find again as they would be in a totally illogical place.

When using a numerical classification, new files are simply given the next number along, although this can create congestion because new files are all together in the same place. Remember that we have already said that new files are usually the most active, which could result in all staff wanting the same files from the same place in the same filing cabinet. Numerical filing systems might use employee or payroll numbers, student enrolment numbers or even telephone numbers to sort information into a logical sequence.

However, this classification is an indirect filing system. In other words it is not possible to go directly to the filing cabinet and remove the file. As it is unlikely that you will be able to remember all identity numbers, an alphabetical index is used. For example, this might store customer details, alphabetically by name. When you need a customer's file, you look through the index for the customer's details and make a note of their identity number.

You then use this number to find the position of their file in the numerical filing system.

■ DIY 1.1.2

Here are the student enrolment numbers for each of the students already sorted alphabetically in DIY 1.1.1. Sort these into numerical order. (Ignore the figures in brackets.)

(1) 178403	(2) 985703	(3) 982649	(4) 815308
(5) 1046892	(6) 876540	(7) 098736	(8) 123428
(9) 234526	(10) 456747	(11) 0345367	(12) 897452
(13) 763490	(14) 173568	(15) 248176	(16) 341098
(17) 909087	(18) 908765	(19) 123456	(20) 987654

Did you notice that two enrolment numbers were longer than the others? Remember that 'nothing' comes before 'something', therefore you should have put the two longest enrolment numbers last.

Subject filing

This is used to keep all information and documents on one subject in the same place. A school teacher or examinations board may use this classification to store their paperwork. Each subject can be subdivided. For example, the English file may be divided into separate divisions under the names of different teachers or examiners. The subject files themselves are kept in alphabetical order, and any sub-

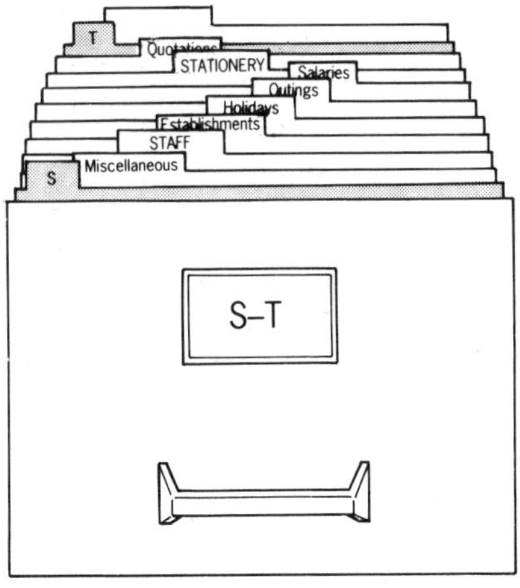

Fig 1.3 A subject filing classification

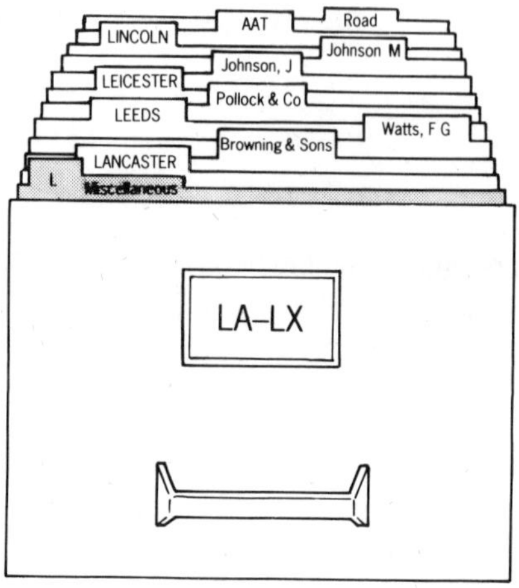

Fig 1.4 A geographical filing classification

divisions within them are also kept alphabetically to help easy retrieval. The main problem with this classification is that regularly-used files can grow too large. This means that retrieval of information may take longer and therefore the efficiency of the system is affected. It is important that subject areas which are expanding quickly are sub-divided to break down the subject into smaller sections. This allows information to be filed in smaller units, which will aid quick and easy retrieval. However, sub-dividing has to be done by someone who understands the system and subject matter very well, in order to ensure that the system is broken down into a logical sequence that all staff understand.

Geographical filing

This arranges names into alphabetical order according to their location. The location can then be sub-divided into smaller areas within that region. Primary guide cards can be used to show the name of the main region, and secondary guide cards to indicate each area within that region. This classification is often used by sales or travel companies who need to keep all information on one area in the same place.

Staff who use this system must have a good working knowledge of the areas and sub-divisions used. A company may divide the files under country, county and town, for example. Staff would be expected to

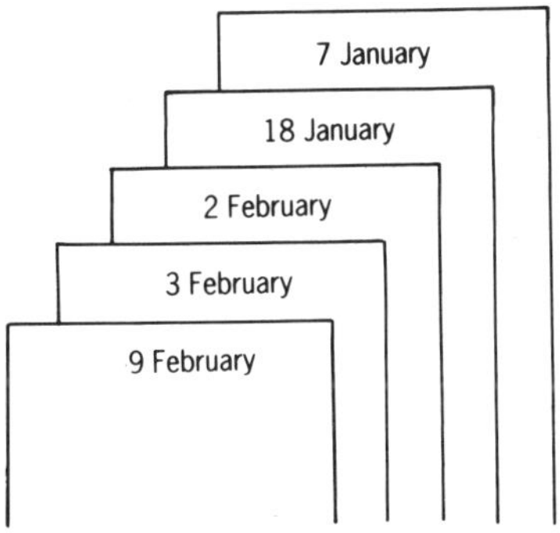

Fig 1.5 A chronological filing classification

recognise that correspondence from Poole would be placed under Dorset which is in England.

Chronological filing

This places material into date order, usually with the earliest date being first. This classification is normally combined with other classifications. For example, documents located in an alphabetical or numerical file would be placed in date order, with the most recent first. Documents such as business letters, memos, price lists and advertising literature are classified in this way so that the most up-to-date material is always at the top of the file.

▶ *How do you sort documents?*

The first thing you must always do is to pre-sort your filing. All this requires is that you go through the filing and sort it into a logical sequence according to the classification used in the office. A concertina folder may be used for pre-sorting, labelled with the same divisions as your filing cabinet (see Fig 1.6). This will enable you to sort all the letters and documents, before they leave your desk, into the order in which they will be placed in the filing cabinet.

Advantages. There are many advantages to this:

1 Once you have found a particular file, you can place all the relevant paperwork inside it – this saves time as you do not have to go back to the same file when more paperwork is found further down the pile of filing.

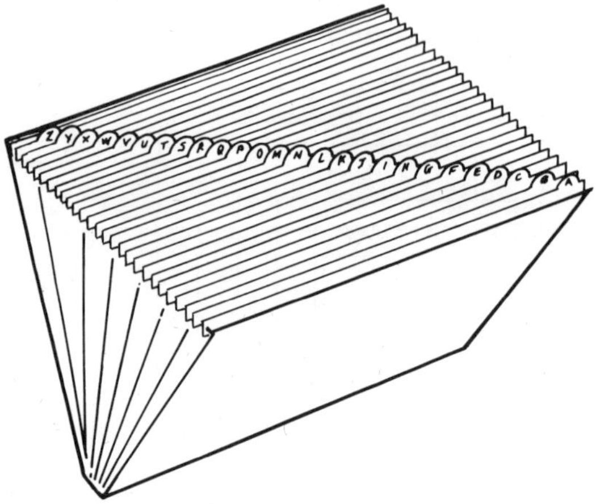

Fig 1.6 A concertina file

2 Once you have opened a cabinet drawer, you will place all paperwork relevant to that drawer into its files – you will not have to jump from drawer to drawer.

3 The time spent filing and when others are prevented from access to the filing cabinet will be reduced.

4 Pre-sorting can be done in your own time and can be slotted in with other duties – because you can take your time, your filing should be more accurate, and documents will be located in the correct place.

5 Paperclips can be removed, documents stapled and damaged paperwork repaired while you are still at your desk.

6 Correspondence for the same file can be sorted into chronological order before you leave your desk.

Once you have pre-sorted the filing, place documents neatly in the file, squarely and not sticking out. Make sure the document is placed into the file and is not allowed to slip between dividers or out of the file itself. If the file is full, divide it into two separate sections, by starting a new file, but make sure you label the new section for easy identification. If there is no file, this may be because the person or business is new and a file will need to be made up, but check with your supervisor first!

▶ *How do you 'open' a new file?*

Most businesses will have new clients, personnel and so on, for whom new files will need to be prepared to hold their forthcoming documentation. In some businesses the job of opening new files is the sole responsibility of the office manager or supervisor, although they may authorise you to do this for them! It is essential, to avoid confusion, that you follow the system already used by the business.

The steps to follow will include some, or all, of the following:

1 Confirm with your supervisor that a new file is required.
2 Confirm the name or number of the new file with the supervisor – also check the required colour coding if this is used.
3 Write or type the name or number of the file directly on to the folder or on to a sticky label – always position this in the same place for each file.
4 Write or type a title strip (if needed) and place this in the correct position in the filing system.
5 Place the folder, complete with contents, in the correct position in the filing cabinet.
6 Write or type an index card, if required.
7 Confirm to your supervisor that the file has been opened and placed into the filing cabinet.

■ DIY 1.1.3

Prepare 20 labels to stick on to folders for the students already sorted in DIY 1.1.1 and 1.1.2. The labels should have the surname in block capitals, followed by a comma and then the first name with initial capital letter. Above the name of each student insert their enrolment number – you will be able to identify these by matching the numbers in the brackets. Present these labels in their correct numerical sequence.

Moving files

It may be necessary to move other files in order to allow space for new files to be slotted in. This is a problem if filing space is limited. It may require folders in a drawer to be moved backwards to allow enough room for a new folder to be inserted. If this means moving files from one drawer to another, remember that a new label will be needed for the front of the filing cabinet drawer to identify its files. The best filing systems offer flexibility and allow expansion of the system as the business grows.

■ DIY 1.1.4

The group of students for whom you have now created labels is called BSIF – FOUNDATION. These folders, when completed, will fill the top drawer of your vertical filing cabinet. Prepare a label to go on the front of the drawer to identify its contents.

▶ *What should you do if unsure of a file's position?*

All business transactions involve keeping records such as letters, invoices, statements and orders, which have to be grouped in some form of logical sequence to allow staff to locate and retrieve them easily. Documentation is said to be the 'backbone' of most businesses. Without quick and reliable methods of classifying material and then storing it in suitable forms for easy retrieval, businesses are unable to function with any degree of efficiency.

If you are ever unsure where to place a file, the first thing to do is to look for clues – look in and around the area of the name or number to see if there are similar files or names. Always look backwards and forwards through files in the cabinet to see if the file has been misplaced. Also, read through the document or correspondence itself to see if there are any other pointers as to where the file may be, it could be under a business name rather than an individual's name!

Only after a thorough search should you ask your supervisor for help. If you show that you have already looked in the more obvious places, your supervisor will not feel that you are wasting time. Bear in mind that office staff may have a slightly different filing system to the one with which you are familiar. It is up to you to familiarise yourself with their system and to ask for assistance when unsure.

Remember that information filed out of place is very difficult to find again and will affect the efficiency of other members of staff and, ultimately, the business itself. There is nothing more frustrating than trying to find a file that has been misplaced by another member of staff. So make sure that person is not you by always asking for assistance if unsure.

▶ *What is an index?*

An index may be provided in many shapes and forms, but its primary use is to provide information quickly and easily. The index itself may contain all the information required – for example, details of medical treatment received at the doctors. Alternatively it may carry selected information, such as the identity number of a customer file which is kept in a numerical filing system. Indexes are used in libraries to assist

Fig 1.7 Card index boxes

with the exact location of books, which may be classified according to the author, title or reference number of the book.

The index that you are most likely to use in an office is a card index.

Card indexes

These are usually kept in small, square, plastic boxes which contain a number of lined postcard-size cards divided by primary guide cards. A separate card is used for each person or business, detailing their address, telephone number and any other relevant information. A second card may be stapled to the first if more space is required. In a library you are likely to find separate index boxes for author, title and reference number. Each card will give exactly the same information, but in a different order. Different coloured cards may be used to identify other information, such as subject area, and cards may be written or typed.

■ DIY 1.1.5

You are now required to prepare an index card for each of the students in the Foundation group (you may use paper cut to postcard size). The index is to be kept in alphabetical order according to surname. Therefore the surname will have to be placed at the top of the card, followed by the student's first name and then their enrolment number. Add the correct address and telephone number to each card. To do this, match the numbers in brackets to your original lists in DIY 1.1.1–1.1.2.

(1)	19 Landers Way, Poole	786578
(2)	12 Tring Place, Bournemouth	789567
(3)	23 Urwin Crescent, Bournemouth	767584
(4)	89 Grenville Road, Poole	765356
(5)	98 Shore Road, Poole	789056
(6)	94 Britannia Road, Poole	734867
(7)	3 Glen Road, Poole	–
(8)	34 Wellington Road, Wareham	680745
(9)	16 Saltash Way, Dorchester	563425
(10)	1 Union Street, Weymouth	234156
(11)	9 Union Street, Weymouth	231769
(12)	56 Oxendon Way, Bournemouth	768598
(13)	76 Somerly Close, Parkstone	764983
(14)	89 Connaught Crescent, Poole	761098

(15)	77 Sunnyside Road, Poole	709164
(16)	1 Salisbury Road, Wareham	680356
(17)	143 Binley Road, Weymouth	–
(18)	19 Penn Hill, Poole	–
(19)	76 Rosey Road, Dorchester	563782
(20)	56 King John Ave, Bournemouth	571880

When you have completed your index cards arrange them in alphabetical order by surname.

▶ *What is a cross-reference?*

It is usual practice to use a cross-reference card or sheet to direct staff to another file for further information. It may be the case that a file could be placed in a number of different locations – a cross-reference card in each location can direct the person to where the actual file is held. A company such as Foster's Footwear would be filed under Foster, but a cross-reference card placed under Footwear would help direct a person quickly to the correct file. A company's name may change or a female member of staff may get married and change her name – both situations require a cross-reference card under the old name to direct the person looking for the file to the right place.

Cross-reference cards, similar to the one in Fig 1.8, are filled in by a member of staff as and when necessary. In the case of a business changing its name or a member of staff changing his/her surname, the old name will be written on the dotted line under 'for correspondence for' and the location of the file on the dotted line under 'see'. If you were opening a new file for James Jones & Co, you might decide to place the file under 'Jones' and a cross-reference card under 'James'.

CROSS-REFERENCE CARD
For correspondence for: ....
See: ....

Fig 1.8 A cross-reference card

DIY 1.1.6

You have just been informed that Jamree Anukot has recently married and her surname has changed to Booker. You will need to amend Jamree's index card so that the surname reads 'Booker', and then file this under 'B'. To prevent any confusion it is also necessary to insert a cross-reference card under 'A' so that anyone looking for Jamree's details under the surname of Anukot will be directed to the correct location.

You have also received some paperwork for Zubeyr Oskara and there appears to be some confusion over which part of his name is the actual surname. To prevent confusion in your index system place a cross-reference card under 'Z' to indicate the correct location of his index card.

▶ *What storage equipment are you likely to use?*

There are three main types of storage equipment used in offices for filing information.

1 Vertical filing cabinets

These are normally made from metal and can be bought as one-, two-, three-, or four-drawer systems. They can be arranged in an office to offer extra worktops or as room dividers. Vertical cabinets allow large quantities of material to be stored in a clean, tidy and organised fashion. The metal cabinets protect their contents from fire and vermin, and, because they can be locked, from unauthorised eyes.

Nowadays, the majority of these cabinets allow folders to sit in suspended pockets that hang from runners along the sides of each drawer. Each pocket is held clear of the bottom of the drawer and can slide backwards and forwards; additional pockets can be inserted easily; and title strips are fixed on the top of each pocket to identify its contents. Pockets can be linked together to form a concertina effect which prevents paperwork dropping between folders, or they may be left to hang loosely, which allows the complete removal of the pocket if necessary.

Material is not, as a general rule, placed directly into the pocket, but is placed into a labelled folder which can sit in the pocket and be removed easily – care must be taken to label clearly both the folder and the pocket title strip. When a file is needed the appropriate drawer is pulled outwards to the relevant point indicated by the title

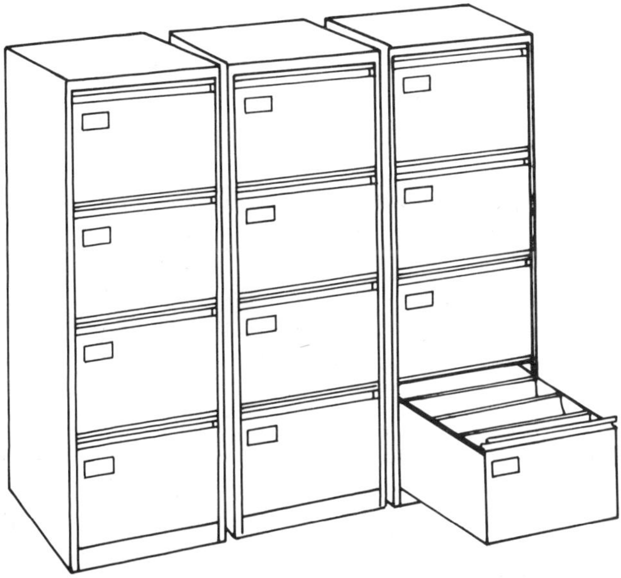

Fig 1.9 Vertical filing cabinets

strip. However, the open drawer can take up a great deal of space and may create problems in a small, busy office.

Care should always be taken not to leave drawers open, as another member of staff may fall over or bump into them, and only one drawer should be opened at a time, to prevent a top-heavy cabinet from falling over. Cabinets may be locked when not in use to protect confidential, private or sensitive information. If you have difficulty in opening a drawer, first check that it has not been locked, and then check to see if one of the other drawers is slightly open. Modern cabinets have an anti-tilt safety device that will prevent you from opening more than one drawer of the cabinet if another drawer is even slightly open!

2 Lateral filing systems

These are used to store material in rows on shelves – like books in a library. This system is space-saving as it requires no extra room to pull out drawers, and can be fitted from floor to ceiling. Shutters or doors can also be added that may be locked when the files are not in use and, therefore, protect confidential material. Pockets can be hung from runners on the underside of shelves and folders can be slotted into each pocket in an upright position. Title strips are attached to the

Fig 1.10 A lateral filing system

side of each pocket to identify its contents – in a similar way to the spine on a book. Folders are easily removed and different sizes of hanging space can be arranged to allow the storage of various sizes of paperwork and documents.

The main disadvantage of this system is that files may become dusty if there is no protective door in use, and files kept at ceiling height are not easily accessible. Special ladders and/or standing stools are required by staff to reach files that are above normal height, and title

Fig 1.11 A horizontal filing system

strips may be difficult to read, as they are hung vertically alongside the pocket.

3 Horizontal filing systems

These allow documents to be stored flat, on top of each other. This method is used for large documents such as maps, drawings and plans, as it allows them to be stored without creasing. The front of each drawer is labelled to identify its contents and the cabinet itself is usually waist-high so that it can be used as a worktop. In general practice, it is unlikely to find such a system of filing unless you are employed in an office such as an architect's, that uses or produces such large, specialised plans and drawings.

There are also smaller types of storage equipment that can be used to protect and keep documents in a logical sequence.

Box files and lever arch files

These files are often used in offices to keep 'pending paperwork' that is waiting for a decision to be made on it. A box file or lever arch file will keep paperwork neat and secure for short or long periods of time.

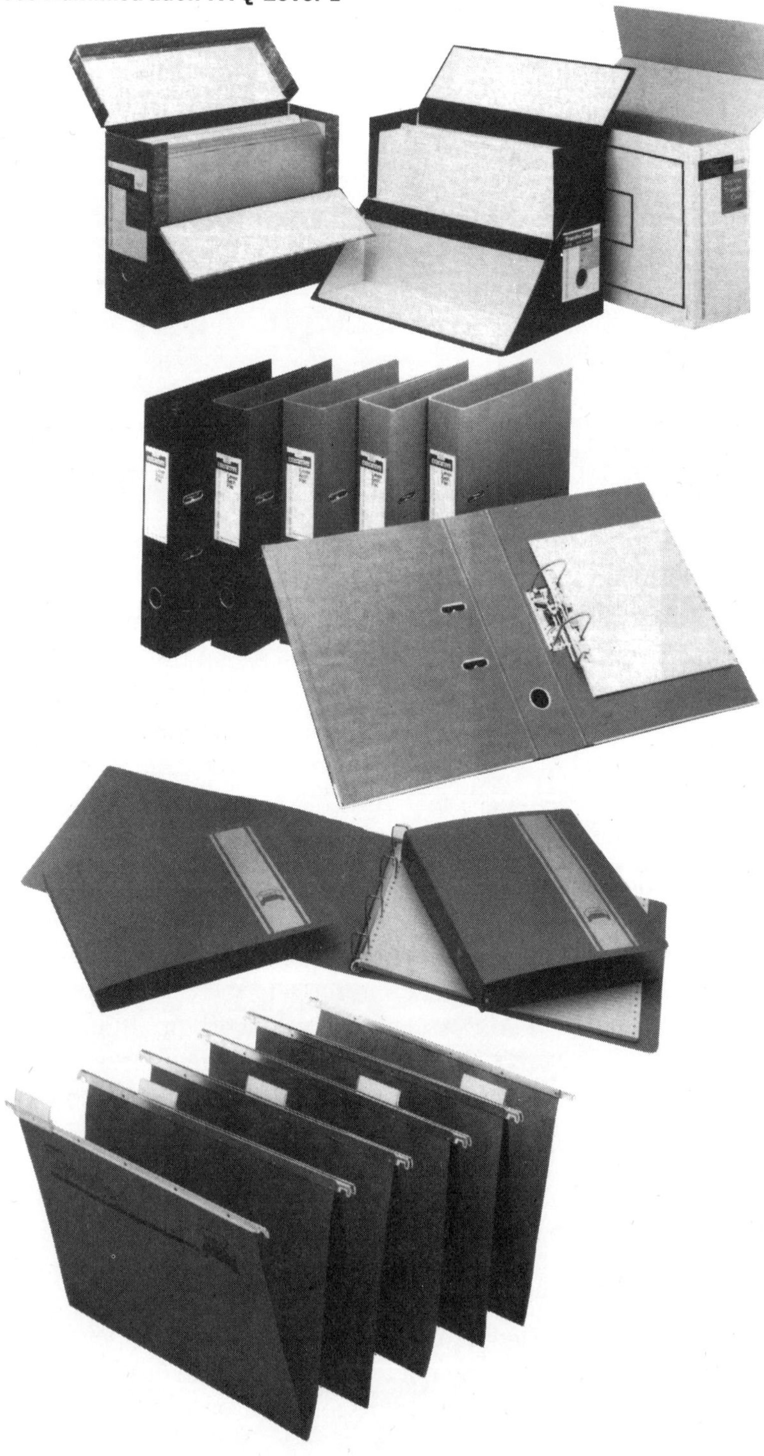

Fig 1.12 Box files, lever arch files, ring binders and pocket folders

Concertina files

These files are also referred to as expanding files because they open out into separate compartments, often labelled with numbers or the letters of the alphabet. These files are useful for pre-sorting documents prior to filing and are often used for storing domestic paperwork such as electricity, gas and telephone bills.

Ring binders

These binders require holes to be punched into the paperwork, or require the use of plastic wallets into which paperwork can be inserted. Guide cards can also be used to divide the information into sections. It is likely that you are currently using such a folder for your coursework.

Pocket folders

These folders are often used to carry paperwork that is stored in a filing cabinet. The flap on the folder helps to keep the contents secure, and the folder can be labelled to indicate its contents. These folders are particularly useful if storing confidential information, as the folder can be clearly marked with the word 'Confidential' and their design helps to keep the enclosed paperwork secure.

Manilla folders

These folders are brown in colour and consist of once piece of folded card. The folder can be labelled and the contents placed inside. When information is required the whole folder can be removed, or just the paperwork required.

▸ *How should you deal with confidential material?*

All business files will contain information that is confidential to a certain degree, such as personal information, financial accounts, minutes from a business meeting or details about the company's future plans. All these would be classified as confidential information.

It is important that you recognise that the information you handle on a daily basis may be routine to you but may be of great value to a rival business. A member of staff may be interested in the salary of a colleague, or perhaps their address and home telephone number.

Therefore, it is important that you do not leave paperwork lying around the office or leave filing drawers open and/or unlocked when you are out of the office.

Make sure that all confidential files are kept in one place, under lock and key, and that folders are marked clearly with the word 'CONFIDENTIAL'. When a confidential file is no longer required, it should not be placed in the bin: the contents of the file should be shredded or burnt in an incinerator so that they do not fall into the wrong hands.

Confidential information held on a computer database must also be protected. This can be done by using passwords or keywords which restrict access. In other words, only those people who are authorised to look at the information will know the password to get into the system. Passwords should be changed regularly and never written down. They can be used to restrict access to a particular computer file or to prevent the actual computer being used in the first place. Some information held on a computer database will be protected under the Data Protection Act, and this is covered on page 112.

▶ *What is a retention policy?*

Each office will have its own retention policy. This is the span of time that documents will be kept in the filing cabinet before being removed and destroyed, or put into long-term storage. Efficiency is about being able to locate and retrieve files quickly. Therefore, filing cabinets have to be 'pruned' regularly and out-of-date documents removed to free space in the cabinet.

Long-term storage may involve the storing of documents in boxes kept in a storeroom or basement. Each box will have to be marked with details of its contents, and again, kept in a logical sequence to aid retrieval if the files are ever needed again.

General correspondence is usually kept for about two years; tax records for six years; share applications for 12 years; patent licences for 30 years; and some legal documents, such as wills, for a person's lifetime. Files may be transferred into long-term storage, or may be destroyed if they are 'dead'. Alternatively, they may be transferred on to microfilm or on to a computer file.

The retention policy for each business will be different, but it is important to know what it is and never to destroy documents without first gaining permission from a supervisor. If a file is 'dead' – in other words, no longer required – then it should be marked accordingly by the supervisor. If you are ever in doubt, ask; it is too late if you have destroyed the wrong document!

■ DIY 1.1.7

Using your own words, complete the following sentences. Do try to write as much as possible in order to prove that you understand everything that has been covered so far.

1 A numerical filing system also needs an alphabetical index because . . .
2 If I were ever unsure of where to file something in an alphabetical system, I would . . . .
3 There are many advantages to pre-sorting documents. Two of these advantages are . . . .
4 If I am unsure of a file's position, I can . . . .
5 Vertical filing cabinets are . . . .
6 A lateral filing system is . . . .
7 When dealing with confidential material, I would always . . . .
8 The retention policy in my organisation is as follows:. . . . .

Completing Element 1.1

To complete this element on filing you will need to put all DIY tasks in your folder, and carry out a final assessment. This must include a minimum of 20 items to be filed on three separate occasions. A different set of documents must be used each time, but you are able to use the index cards completed in DIY 1.1.5 as one set. Included in the assessment must be the introduction of at least two new files to the system, unmarked, and unclearly-marked items.

If you are responsible at work for filing, you will be able to get credit by showing your tutor or assessor what you do. To do this, complete a log over a period of time detailing all your filing activities.

Claiming credit

Once you have completed your final assessment, you will need to write in your record book or folder *how, when, where* and *what* you have done to prove that you are competent.

The following is an example of how one trainee completed this claim:

1.1.a While on work placement at Coopers and Co, from 5.5.9– to 23.5.9–, I filed all documents in the right place as quickly as possible.

1.1.b I made sure all damaged paperwork was repaired, paperclips removed, and paperwork placed flat and square in the folder. I always closed the cabinet drawer when I had finished.

1.1.c I used an alphabetical system in the personnel department and a numerical system in the accounts department. I always made sure documents were put in the right place.

1.1.d If I was ever unsure of where to put a document, I always asked my supervisor for help.

■ Element 1.2

IDENTIFY AND RETRIEVE DOCUMENTS FROM WITHIN AN ESTABLISHED FILING SYSTEM

Do you know where documents such as your birth certificate, medical card or school/work reference are kept? These papers have to be kept because the information they hold will be needed at some future date. Filing, if carried out efficiently, will ensure that when such documents are required they will be found quickly and easily. Imagine if you had to keep all the above documents for everyone in your class or office – do you think you would be able to find each document quickly? The answer to this question will only be 'yes' if you have kept these documents in a logical sequence.

Filing means storing information so that it can be found when it is wanted. Organisations keep large quantities of information on file that may be referred to regularly or, possibly, on a one-off basis. However, what is important is that, while all information must be kept secure, it must also be readily and easily available for use, regardless of how 'active' it is. A good filing system will preserve and protect information and at the same time present it in a logical and easily-accessible manner. In order to prevent files being mislaid, it is vital that staff understand the procedure in use and follow the office rules for filing.

There are certain filing terms which you must understand.

▶ *Release symbols*

Some offices have trays into which staff place documents that are ready to be filed away. Different trays may be supplied for different departments and subjects, or it may be the case that one tray is used for all filing. Whichever method is used, it is important that trays are emptied regularly and filing kept up to date. If at any point you have a query, place this in a separate tray and deal with it once you have completed the rest of the filing.

Some organisations use special marks or 'release symbols' to show that a document is ready for filing. A line across the page from corner to corner, the word 'FILE' written or stamped on to the document, or a simple 'F' in one corner are all examples of the marks used to show that the document should now be filed. If you are given a document without a release symbol, put it into the query tray so that it may be returned to the relevant department and a release symbol added if required.

It is usual practice for office staff to indicate under what name they want the document to be filed. Staff may circle or underline wording on the document that shows where it should be filed. Alternatively, they will write on the document itself the name under which the document should be filed. If you are ever in doubt, go back to the person who has released the document and ask for assistance. A document placed in the wrong file is very difficult to find and could well be lost forever!

▶ *Absent folders*

When a file is removed from the filing cabinet, it is important to keep track of who has the file and to which department or office it has been taken. It is also important for you to know the date of removal, and the date of the file's return to the filing system. An absent folder can be used to detail all this information and this folder is placed in the space left by the missing file. When another member of staff wants the missing file, they are able to see who has it and, therefore, can go straight to that person and ask for its return.

If an absent folder is used, documents for the missing file can be placed in the folder and then moved across when the original file is returned. By looking at the date the file was removed, you will have a

ABSENT FOLDER

Date taken	Name/Number of file taken	Taken by	Date returned

Fig 1.13 An absent folder

good idea of whether the file should have been returned. If the same person keeps the file for a number of weeks and documents are piling up in the absent folder, you should request the return of file for up-dating.

Most organisations use a printed form, similar to the one in Fig 1.13, which can be glued on to the front or back of an empty folder. The folder used will normally be the same size and type as those already used in the filing system, although a different colour may be used to show that it is an absent folder. The person taking the original file must complete the details required on the printed form and put the absent folder in place of the original file. When the original folder is returned the absent folder can be removed and used again elsewhere.

▶ *Out cards*

If you are responsible for the filing in your office, you will also take on the responsibility for lending out files or individual documents. It is important that you keep track of who has what. If one piece of paperwork or a separate document is removed from a file, this must be replaced with an out card detailing the name of the borrower, department, date borrowed and date returned. It is important to

OUT CARD				
Document title	Borrower	Department	Date borrowed	Date returned

Fig 1.14 An out card

include details of the title of the document or paperwork so that, in the event of it being mislaid, you have a description of what it was.

You will find that some organisations use absent folders and out cards, some will use one or the other and some will not bother with either! If you are responsible for the filing, you will be expected to know where files have gone and who has taken missing paperwork. The efficient way to do this is to complete an absent folder when a complete file is taken and an out card when individual documents or paperwork are removed from a folder. Absent folders and out cards should be kept in a convenient place near to the filing system to encourage their use by all members of staff.

■ DIY 1.2.1

Draw up an A4 sheet of paper that can be glued or otherwise attached to a folder to make it into an absent folder, and insert the following information:

1 On 10 January Mrs M Protheroe of the Personnel Department borrowed the file of Mr D Carmichael. The file was returned on the 12 January.

2 On 18 January Miss Sheryl Byworth, Sales Manageress, borrowed the file of G Mackett & Son. The file was returned one week later.

3 On 26 January Mrs Lynne Wheeler, Head of Computing, borrowed the file on H Todd & Co Business Systems, and returned it on the same day.

4 On 27 January Mr P D Stott, General Manager, borrowed the confidential file on Mr Jeremy DeVille, which has not yet been returned.

Mrs Protheroe from Personnel has asked you to locate and retrieve the confidential file on Mr Jeremy DeVille, as she needs it for his interview on Wednesday of next week. Write a memo to Mr Stott requesting that he return the file immediately.

▶ *A bring-forward system?*

This is also called a reminder system or a tickler file. Many documents have to be followed up, bills paid by a specified date, reminder letters sent, and so on. These all require action when a particular date is reached, which may be in the near future, or perhaps a year or more away. It is important that some form of reminder system is used to tell staff that a certain task now needs to be completed. A simple way of doing this is to use a desk diary, with entries made for dates in the future to act as reminders.

However, a tickler file or bring-forward system can be used to provide

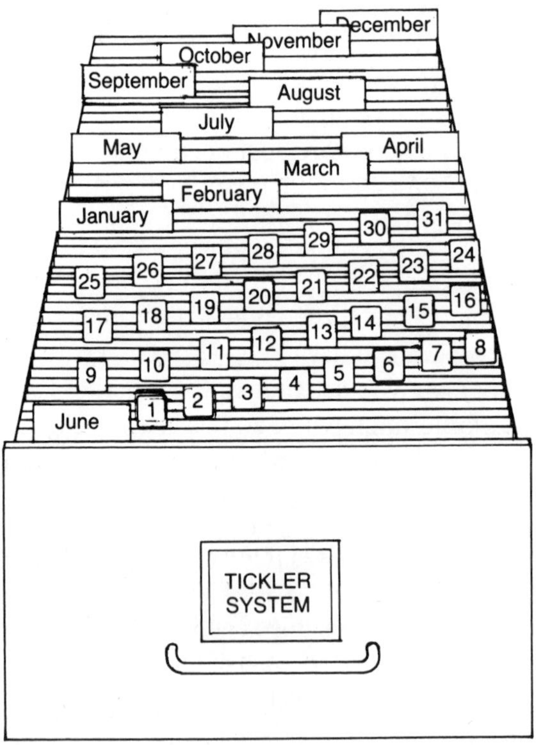

Fig 1.15 A tickler file (bring-forward system)

staff with a monthly, day-by-day account of jobs to be done. The system consists of 12 guide cards, one for each month of the year. The current month will have 31 separate cards dividing the month into days. Each of these sections will contain details of jobs to be done on that particular day, reminders of correspondence to be sent out or perhaps information that needs to be 'chased up'.

When letters are received or appointments made that require some future activity, a dated reminder is placed in the appropriate month. When that month is reached and becomes the current month, the 31 day cards are moved behind the guide card for that month. All reminders are then sorted into date order and placed into the relevant slot in the file.

Examples of people who would use this system are:

- Vets, to remind a pet's owner when annual injections are due.
- Doctors, to check when a patient's repeat prescriptions are due.
- Accounts staff, to remind them when their clients' annual accounts have to be prepared and VAT returns paid.
- Travel agents, to remind them to notify customers that full payment for their holiday is now due.

▶ *How will you work to deadlines?*

Suppose that you are called out of the office to help to complete an urgent project in another office. The task you thought you would complete in five minutes has turned out to be more complicated than you thought. Several files you have been asked to locate have disappeared (the person who has them did not bother to complete the absent folders!). Another member of staff is ill and you find yourself also having to answer their telephone and deal with their visitors. Finally you realise that you will not get the filing completed by the end of the day.

This situation is not unrealistic. The daily requirements of an office can never be anticipated, and a telephone call from a member of staff to say they are ill, a breakdown of machinery, or a job to be completed urgently could all affect your routine for the day.

Efficiency is about working to deadlines and reallocating priorities! Just when you think you have organised your working day to complete all the work in your in-tray, something can happen to throw you off target. You will find you are having to reorganise tasks according to their level of priority – in other words, the most important need to be done first. Tasks that can be left until tomorrow will have to be rescheduled, although it is wise to remember that the longer these tasks take to complete, the more of a priority they become as their deadline moves nearer!

If at any time you feel you will not get your work done as soon as you had planned, it is important that you tell your supervisor. It is always better to offer an alternative – explain why the job has not been done, but that you will be able to complete it first thing tomorrow. If you are totally overwhelmed with work, your supervisor may be able to bring in some extra help to assist you. Do not try to take on more and more work if you find yourself falling behind. Tell your supervisor what is happening as it may have gone unnoticed that you have more work than you can cope with in the time available.

If you give your work colleagues fair warning of any unavoidable delay, they will understand and may even be able to suggest an alternative to help you out. If you do not let colleagues know, they are more likely to be annoyed and blame you for not completing routine tasks.

■ DIY 1.2.2

It is Friday morning and you have decided to do the week's filing. You would normally do this on a daily basis, but as you have been covering for the receptionist, who is on holiday, your own work has fallen behind. While you are sitting at your desk pre-sorting the week's filing, Lucy Frazer from accounts asks you where a client's paperwork has gone, as she cannot find it in the file. You tell her you are just pre-sorting the week's filing and that you will try to locate her client's paperwork. She is very angry with this delay, as her client is seated waiting in the office, and she tells you that she intends to make an official complaint.

You are very upset by Lucy's comments and decide to write a memo to your own boss, Mrs N Vincent in Personnel, to explain to her why you have not been able to complete the week's filing. You wish to explain to her that the filing was not done as regularly as usual because you were covering the reception and did not have enough time. You also want to bring it to her notice that you placed absent folders and out cards on top of the filing cabinets for staff to complete when removing files or paperwork. If an out card had been completed by the person taking the paperwork from the folder of Lucy Frazer's client, this could have been easily located!

What is a miscellaneous file?

It is important not to tie up valuable space in the filing system by opening files for one-off pieces of information. It may be the case that a business or person has placed an order, sent an enquiry or perhaps made a complaint. In each of these cases, once the matter has been dealt with, the person or business may not be contacted again. It is usual practice to place such paperwork in a miscellaneous file until it has been established whether or not the person or business will generate more paperwork, and therefore will need to open a new file.

A miscellaneous file should be placed at the beginning of each new section in the filing system, under A, B, C, and so on (see Fig 1.1). Paperwork placed in the folder should also be in alphabetical order. The folder can be used to hold non-routine or special paperwork while awaiting guidance on its full classification or the need for a folder of its own.

■ DIY 1.2.3

Below, you will find sentences that are incomplete. The sentences are relevant to work already covered. Copy out these sentences and fill in the missing word(s), which you can select from the following lists.

1 *easily securely storing wanted readily*

2 *logical preserve accessible protect*

3 *policy pruned retention*

4 *symbols file release*

5 *vets monthly doctors reminder accountants tickler*

6 *warning deadlines unavoidable important reallocating*

1 Filing means _ _ _ _ _ _ _ _ information so that it can be found when _ _ _ _ _ _. It is important that information is kept _ _ _ _ _ _ _ _, but at the same time it must be _ _ _ _ _ _ _ _ and _ _ _ _ _ _ available for use.

2 A good filing system will _ _ _ _ _ _ _ _ _ and _ _ _ _ _ _ _ _ information and at the same time present it in a _ _ _ _ _ _ _ _ and easily _ _ _ _ _ _ _ _ _ manner.

3 The span of time that documents will be kept in the filing cabinet before being removed is ruled by the organisation's _ _ _ _ _ _ _ _ _ _   _ _ _ _ _ _. Filing cabinets have to be _ _ _ _ _ _ regularly to free space.

4 Some businesses use _ _ _ _ _ _ _ _   _ _ _ _ _ _ _ _ to show that a document is ready for filing. A line across a document or the word '_ _ _ _' written or stamped on the front page are examples.

5 A bring-forward system is also called a _ _ _ _ _ _ _ _ _ system or a _ _ _ _ _ _ _ _ file. It is used to provide staff with a _ _ _ _ _ _ _ _, day-by-day account of jobs to be done. This type of system would be used by people such as _ _ _ _, _ _ _ _ _ _ _ _ and _ _ _ _ _ _ _ _ _ _ _ _ _ as a reminder of jobs to be done on a particular day.

6 Efficiency is about working to _ _ _ _ _ _ _ _ _ _ and _ _ _ _ _ _ _ _ _ _ _ _ _ _ priorities. This means reorganising your day to make sure the most _ _ _ _ _ _ _ _ _ _ _ tasks are completed first. You should always give colleagues fair _ _ _ _ _ _ _ _ of _ _ _ _ _ _ _ _ _ _ _ _ _ delays so they are given an opportunity to reallocate their own priorities.

Completing Element 1.2

To complete this element on filing you will need to put all DIY tasks in your folder, and carry out a final assessment. This must cover a minimum of 20 items to be extracted from a filing system on a minimum of three separate occasions. A completely different set of documents must be used each time, but you are able to use the index cards completed for DIY 1.1.5 as one set. If you are responsible at work for filing, you will be able to get credit by showing your tutor or assessor what you do. To do this, complete a log over a period of time detailing all your filing activities – you must also include details of occasions when you have had to reallocate priorities.

Claiming credit

Once you have completed your final assessment, you will need to write in your record book or folder *how, when, where* and *what* you have done to prove that you are competent.

The following is an example of how one trainee completed this claim:

1.2.a While on work placement at Coopers and Co, from 5.5.9–to 23.5.9–, I located documents quickly and accurately. I took the documents to the department or person who had asked for them.

1.2.b If I could not locate a document, I would ask the supervisor for help and explain why I was having difficulty. If this meant there would be a delay, I explained this to the person who had asked for the file.

1.2.c I completed an assignment at college where I had to record file movements by filling in an out card. I kept the out card up to date, neat and accurate. (See work folder for evidence.)

UNIT 2
Communicating information

Element 2.1
PROCESS INCOMING AND OUTGOING BUSINESS TELEPHONE CALLS

Modern telephone systems have been designed to meet the needs of an organisation of any size. A switchboard may be used that allows a number of incoming calls to be connected and then transferred to the relevant person or department. Internal telephones allow members of staff to make direct contact with each other, using an internal telephone extension number. They also allow contact with the main switchboard, which may have to be used to request an outside line in order to make an external telephone call.

You will find that all organisations, whatever their size, depend upon telephone contact. Some conduct a major part of their business over the telephone, for example, orders for goods from a mail-order catalogue. They rely on well-trained members of staff to answer and record information quickly, efficiently and accurately. Mistakes cost time and money and will not be tolerated by a business organisation. In an emergency situation, mistakes might even cost lives.

When members of staff answer the telephone, they act as representatives of that organisation and therefore must create the right impression. Staff have a responsibility to communicate information accurately and clearly, using an appropriate style, tone and vocabulary. Good communication skills are essential if this is to be achieved. A member of staff who sounds competent, efficient and gives a good impression of the organisation over the telephone is a valuable addition.

Fig 2.1 An office telephone

▶ *What equipment are you likely to use?*

There is a range of telecommunications equipment available to suit the demands of each organisation. This depends on the size of the organisation and the department in which you work. You may find yourself using a telephone switchboard with up to 10 incoming lines and numerous internal extensions; or you may be responsible for using an office telephone with a single, direct line out or linked to a main switchboard.

Telephone

Modern telephones offer numerous additional facilities, such as last number redial, memory, selective call-barring, secrecy. They also offer diversion services, such as no-reply diversion or engaged diversion, three way service and call waiting. There are other facilities and services available, some of which are free although others will be charged for. It is important that you understand the facilities available on the telephones you use at work (and at home) and appreciate how these might be used to improve your efficiency when at work.

■ DIY 2.1.1

Look at the facilities available on your telephone, at work, in the training centre, or at home. List each service and explain how to operate it and why it might be used. Draw a diagram of the keypad on your telephone, and draw arrows to indicate the buttons used for each facility. The sales book that accompanied the telephone will give this information, but if this has been misplaced you may like to ask your supervisor, your parents, or contact BT for information.

Explain why call-barring and call waiting may be used.

Switchboard

A switchboard is used to accept incoming calls, allow them to be answered and then transferred to the appropriate person or department. Calls can be held or 'parked' while the switchboard operator deals with other calls, locates a particular person or finds out information. Switchboards can be used to monitor all outgoing external calls made by members of staff. They will need to request an

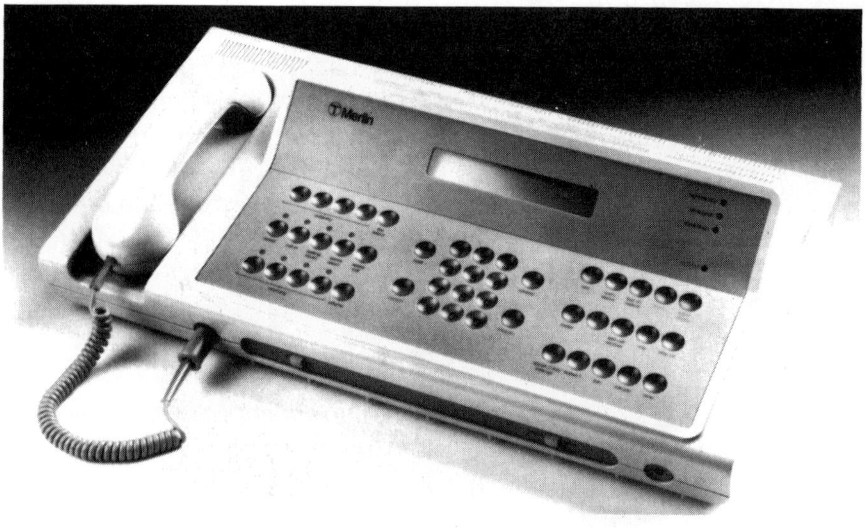

Fig 2.2 An electronic switchboard

outside line from the switchboard operator before they can dial out. Some switchboards require the operator to dial the number and then transfer the call to the member of staff once it is connected. Other switchboards can be set up to allow for extensions to have direct access to an outside line by dialing a number, eg 9.

Switchboards can be programmed to prevent long-distance calls being made during the peak rate hours of 0900–1300 hours. This encourages staff to make more expensive, long-distance calls during the standard rate hours of 0800–0900 hours and 1300–1800 hours. Cheap rate calls can be made from midnight to 0800 hours and 1800 hours to midnight. Saturday and Sunday are charged at cheap rate. Internal calls made within an organisation are free of charge as they are operated through the organisation's own switchboard.

Answering machines

These machines are used to answer the telephone when no-one is available, ensuring that no calls or messages are missed. An announcement is recorded which invites the caller to leave a message after the 'bleep'. Answering machines allow the office to be unattended while orders and messages are left, recorded on the machine, during any time of the day or night.

If you are answered by an answering machine, do not be frightened. Speak slowly and clearly, stating your business and remembering to

Fig 2.3 An answerphone

leave your name and telephone number. It is also wise to state the date and time of day that you are calling. If you do find yourself surprised by an answering machine, replace your receiver, write down your message and call back when you have prepared yourself.

The first person in the office in the morning should play the recorded messages to find out if there is anything important that needs attention straight away. When the tape is played back it is wise to have a pen and paper ready to jot down all information and telephone numbers.

■ DIY 2.1.2

1 You have been given the job of recording the announcement to be played on your organisation's answering machine. On a piece of paper write down word for word what you will say. You will now have to record the announcement, either using a cassette recorder or an answering machine. Keep the cassette as evidence of what you have done.

2 You have been given details of the charge bands used by BT to calculate telephone charges. (They are shown in the text above.) In their present form they are a little difficult to understand. Design a poster on A4 paper displaying in an easily understood format the three different charge bands. The poster is to be displayed in the office to remind staff when it is cheapest to use the telephone.

▶ *How should a telephone be answered?*

1 A ringing telephone should be answered as quickly as possible (some organisations guarantee that your call will be answered in no more than four rings!).
2 Identify the organisation and yourself clearly (organisations will have an approved method of doing this).
3 Use a pen and paper to note all information.
4 Identify the caller and either deal with the call yourself or transfer the caller to someone who can help (announce the name of the caller before transferring the call to the other person).
5 Always remain courteous, polite and above all, helpful.
6 Keep the caller informed of your actions so they are aware of any delay and never tell a caller to 'hang on'.

7 If the call is for someone who is not available, ask if anyone else can help; if not, take a message.
8 Do not give confidential information; pass the call to your supervisor.
9 If you do not have the requested information at hand, offer to ring the caller back.
10 Before ringing off, make sure you have recorded all the information required, including the caller's telephone number (you may also have to complete a log book of all incoming calls).

■ DIY 2.1.3

Design a log sheet on a piece of A4 paper that can be used to record all incoming calls received and dealt with by you. The sheet will need details such as date and time, name of caller (together with the name of the organisation if relevant), brief details of the request and the action taken. If you have taken a message for someone, keep a copy of the message and attach this to the back of your log sheet. When you have completed 15 entries, ask your supervisor to sign the sheet to confirm that you have proved your competence.

▶ *How would you deal with a wrong number?*

First try to help the caller. Give your own organisation's number again to clarify where the mistake has been made. If your number is different to that required, the caller can ring off and dial the correct number. If the caller has been given your organisation's number by mistake, ask for more details about the enquiry and see if you can find the correct number.

If you find that you regularly receive calls for another organisation, keep a note of its number so that it can be passed on to the caller quickly and efficiently. Never be off-hand with a caller who has the wrong number, but be polite and helpful as this will create a good impression of your own organisation. You may find that you receive a lot of wrong number calls because your number is similar to that of another organisation, or above or below their number in the directory. If you greet callers correctly and give a good impression you may attract additional business.

▶ *How would you ensure a message is taken accurately?*

Firstly, remember to keep pen or pencil, scrap paper and telephone message pad next to the telephone. You will need to pass on the following information:

1 Name of caller and organisation/department
2 Caller's telephone and extension number
3 Details of message
4 Name/department/room number of person for whom the message is intended
5 Date and time of call
6 Your name as the receiver of the call

You may prefer to write information received over the telephone on to scrap paper and then transfer this neatly to the message pad. If you are busy, however, it may be safer to write directly on to the message pad so that you do not forget the call. It is vitally important that messages are passed on promptly to the correct person so that the call can be returned. Do not leave messages lying around on your desk. A lost message to return a call could mean a lost order for business and a very angry colleague.

When you have taken a message, you should always confirm the details by reading them back to the caller. Repeat the name and contact number to ensure that mistakes have not been made. One wrong digit in a telephone number will cause confusion and create a bad impression of your organisation if the call cannot be returned. Messages must give full information. It is not acceptable to write that 'a man called...', or, 'I think her name was...'. If you are ever unsure of what a caller has said, do not be afraid to ask him/her to repeat details or spell out words you do not understand.

Page 59 shows the telephone alphabet which can be used to clarify information over the telephone.

■ DIY 2.1.4

Read through the following telephone conversation.

You Good morning, Coopers and Co. How may I help you?

Caller Hello, My name is Jones and I would like to speak with your Personnel Manager.

MESSAGE FOR

M ______________________________

WHILE YOU WERE OUT

M ______________________________

Of ______________________________

Telephone No ______________________________

Telephoned		Please ring	
Called to see you		Will call again	
Wants to see you		Urgent	

Message: ______________________________

Date ______________ Time ______________

Received by ______________________________

Fig 2.4 A telephone message form

You I'm afraid she is out of the office this morning. Would you like to speak with her secretary?

Caller No, I have already left messages with her secretary twice and have not received a return call.

You I'm terribly sorry. Would you like to leave details of your message with me and I will ensure that our Personnel Manager, Mrs Drake, gets it as soon as she arrives back this afternoon.

Caller Well, if I must. It really is quite urgent. My name is Jones, Mr Patrick Jones, and I would like to be sent an application form for the position of assistant caretaker. My address is 36 Norton Road, Plymouth, Devon, postcode PL1 2UH. My telephone number is 345274 and I would like to discuss the vacancy with the Personnel Manager before making my application.

You That's fine Mr Jones, I'll pass the message to Mrs Drake as soon as she arrives back in her office and ask her to call you on 345274.

Caller Thank you, and I do hope she gets my message this time. Goodbye.

You I can assure you she will Mr Jones. Thank you. Goodbye.

1 Complete a message slip detailing all relevant information – use today's date and the current time.

2 You have just been informed that Mrs Drake will be away for the next two weeks and will not be returning to the office this afternoon. Is there anyone else who can speak to Mr Jones about the vacancy? If so, write a message slip for him/her.

▶ *What information can be given over the telephone?*

The amount of information you are able to give over the telephone will increase as you get to know the organisation for which you work. It is important, however, that you recognise occasions when information should or should not be given out. You have already been told that you must be polite and helpful at all times, but this does not mean giving out any information you can lay your hands on in the name of helpfulness.

If you are ever unsure, tell the caller that you do not have the information and that you will transfer them to your supervisor. Alternatively, offer to call them back later, to give you time to check. It is important for you to realise that limitations governing disclosable information are there to protect the organisation, its business and its employees.

You will learn from the organisation's literature, such as house journals, organisation charts, internal telephone directories, catalogues, price lists. You will also learn by talking to members of staff about their role and duties in the organisation. With experience, you will know about the products or services offered by the organisation, which departments deal with different areas of work and who to contact if a person is not available.

■ DIY 2.1.5

How good are you at finding out information? Give the answers to the following questions together with details of where you found this information. If you feel the information requested is confidential, explain the reason why.

1 Name of the most senior person in your organisation, eg Chairman, Principal.
2 What products/services does the organisation offer?
3 Name and extension number of the Health and Safety Representative.
4 Name and address of your Department Head.
5 Name, address and telephone number of your organisation's stationery suppliers.
6 Name and extension number of the member of staff to be called in an emergency.
7 The BT number giving advice on how to deal with nuisance calls.
8 The address and home telephone number of your immediate boss.
9 Details of the organisation's last VAT or tax returns.
10 The organisation's fax number.
11 The BT number used to request a leaflet giving tips on how to use the telephone correctly (*Be Your Own Boss*).
12 Explain the structure of the organisation.

▶ *How do you make an outgoing call?*

We all think we know how to use the telephone, but it is surprising how easily mistakes can be made. By following a few simple rules, you can avoid making mistakes and help build your confidence.

1 Write down the number and dialling code (check these are correct) and the name or the department that you require.
2 Make a list of questions or notes needed for the call.
3 Lift the receiver and listen for the dial tone (you may have a hands-free button that allows you to talk into a small speaker and keep both hands free).

4 Key in the full number carefully at a steady rate (a beep will be heard each time a number is accepted).
5 If you make a mistake, replace the receiver, wait a couple of seconds and try again.
6 When the call is answered, ask for the person or department required, and/or the extension number, if known; give your own name and/or the name of your organisation, and say on whose behalf you are calling, if this is relevant.
7 When you are connected, be prepared to repeat the same information again.
8 Talk clearly and concisely, using your notes as a reminder to ensure that you do not forget anything.
9 If the call is for your boss, explain this to the person and then transfer the call, making sure you first announce their name to your boss.
10 If you are cut off, as you are the caller it is your responsibility to call again.

Costs in time and money can be reduced if calls are kept to the point and made during standard rate times.

■ DIY 2.1.6

Design on a piece of A4 paper a log sheet that can be used to record all outgoing calls dealt with by you. The sheet will need details such as date and time; name of the person you are calling (together with the name of the organisation, if relevant); telephone number; and brief details of the purpose for the call. When you have completed 15 entries, ask your supervisor to sign the sheet to confirm that you have proved yourself competent.

▶ *What sources of information are available?*

You will inevitably use a BT *Phone Book* for your local area, together with *Yellow Pages* and *The Thomson Local Directory*. Use these books to find local telephone numbers, area codes, addresses and even postcodes for business and private users.

Business Pages (similar to *Yellow Pages*) is used by business suppliers and covers a wider area but does not cover retail outlets and services.

Your organisation should also have an Internal Directory giving details of all personnel, departments and extension numbers. This should, in addition, give details of frequently-used external numbers, eg branch offices, so that staff do not use BT's Directory Enquiries, which would incur charges.

The only free BT information service still available is the speaking clock sponsored by Accurist. All other services are offered by private companies, who make a charge for the service. These services are usually advertised in newspapers and start with the prefix 0891. The Freefone service does not provide information but does encourage potential customers to ring free of charge using a 0800 number.

Remember that there are other companies, such as Mercury, that supply telecommunications equipment and services in competition with BT.

■ DIY 2.1.7

Use the BT local *Phone Book* to find numbers for:

1 Requesting information about BT's products and services for disabled customers
2 The International Operator
3 Directory Enquiries
4 International Directory Enquiries
5 Reporting a fault for a personal customer
6 Reporting a fault for a business customer
7 Your nearest Police Station
8 Requesting a copy of the *International Telephone Guide*
9 Aruba and Liechtenstein (international codes)
10 Your nearest airport

Use the *Phone Book* to calculate the time difference between:

1 London and Moscow
2 London and Sydney
3 London and New York

▶ *What about international calls?*

Most international calls can be made using IDD (International Direct Dialling), but if problems are encountered the International Operator can be contacted on 155 for assistance. Your answer to question 8 above will give you a number to call free of charge to request an *International Telephone Guide* from BT – it would be wise for you to do this now if you have not already done so!

The International Operator will not only help with international calls but can also give you a demonstration of the tones which you can expect to hear when calling internationally.

Remember that international calls are charged at a higher rate than domestic calls and, therefore, it is important that you choose carefully the time of day when you make your call. You can use the *Phone Book*, International Time Zones page, to calculate the time difference between Britain and the country you wish to contact.

▶ *How do you maintain security?*

The first thing to remember is to use your discretion – if you are ever unsure, ask your supervisor. You will find that during your working duties you will have access to many types of information. It may just be part of a day's work to you but the information you deal with could be very sensitive and of use to other people or organisations. Be helpful, but never disclose information to others that may be considered confidential by your organisation.

Personnel and wages records, financial and medical reports, and information such as sales and profit reports, are examples of records that contain information that should not be given to callers. Think how you would feel if your name, address and personal details were given to 'someone' over the telephone. Would you like to think that other people were given information about your bank account or medical details?

▶ *What about emergencies?*

In the event of an emergency, using the telephone could save someone's life. In order to be effective in an emergency you must know the correct procedure to follow. Do you contact your supervisor or main switchboard operator first? Will you be able to call the emergency services yourself if it is a matter of life or death?

Remember that some telephones will not have access to an outside line and you may have to go through the organisation's switchboard, who will call the emergency services on your behalf. Some organisations have their own internal emergency number, eg 222, which will be answered immediately by the switchboard operator.

If you do have to call the emergency services yourself, be prepared with the relevant information:

- Dial 999
- Which service do you require? Fire, Police or Ambulance? (You might even need Coast Guard, Mountain or Cave Rescue)
- Give the name and address of your organisation
- Give your own name and position in the organisation
- Give brief details of the emergency
- Do not ring off until told to do so

It is vital that you know what to do in an emergency – if you are unsure, now is the time to ask your supervisor.

▶ *What about safety?*

Using the telephone should not be a dangerous activity, but safety rules still apply.

1 Do not trail wires across the floor or walkway
2 Keep the earpiece and mouthpiece of your telephone clean
3 Do not eat or drink over telecommunications equipment
4 Keep the telephone in an accessible place
5 Do not sit on desk tops while using the telephone
6 Use ample extensions for the number of people in the office

■ DIY 2.1.8

Read through the information below and insert the following missing words where required.
message / mistakes / date / standard / peak / another / digit / long-distance / answering / repeat / helpful / call / time / impression / clearly / efficiently / spell / cheap / representative / accurately / wrong

1 When a member of staff answers the telephone he/she acts as a _ _ _ _ _ _ _ _ _ _ _ _ _ _ _ for the organisation and therefore must create the right _ _ _ _ _ _ _ _ _ _. Staff have a responsibility to communicate information _ _ _ _ _ _ _ _ _ _ _ and clearly, using an appropriate style, tone and vocabulary.

2 Switchboards can be programmed to prevent _ _ _ _ - _ _ _ _ _ _ _ _ _ calls being made during _ _ _ _ rate hours of 0900–1300 hours. This encourages staff to make more expensive, long-distance calls during the _ _ _ _ _ _ _ _ _ rate hours of 0800–0900 hours and 1300–1800 hours. _ _ _ _ _ rate calls can be made from midnight to 0800 hours and 1800 hours to midnight.

3 If you are answered by an _ _ _ _ _ _ _ _ _ _ machine, do not be frightened. Speak slowly and _ _ _ _ _ _ _, stating your business, and remember to leave your name and telephone number. It is also wise to state the _ _ _ _ and _ _ _ _ of day that you are calling.

4 When you have taken a _ _ _ _ _ _ _ _ you should always confirm the details to the caller. Repeat the name and contact number to ensure that _ _ _ _ _ _ _ _ _ have not been made. One wrong _ _ _ _ _ in a telephone number will cause much confusion and create a bad impression of your organisation if the _ _ _ _ cannot be returned. If you are ever unsure of what a caller has said, do not be afraid to ask them to _ _ _ _ _ _ details or _ _ _ _ _ out words you do not understand.

5 If you find that you regularly receive calls for _ _ _ _ _ _ _ _ organisation, keep a note of its number so that this can be passed on to the caller quickly and _ _ _ _ _ _ _ _ _ _ _ _. Never be off-hand with a caller who has the _ _ _ _ _ number. Be polite and _ _ _ _ _ _ _ _ as this will create a good impression of your own organisation.

Completing Element 2.1

To complete this element on processing incoming and outgoing business telephone calls you will need to put all the DIY tasks in your work folder. If you have demonstrated competence by dealing with a minimum of 10 consecutive incoming and outgoing calls on a minimum of three separate occasions, you will have evidence of this on the log sheets completed for DIY 2.1.3 and 2.1.6. If you do not have enough evidence, you will need to carry out a final assessment to cover the above evidence required for this element.

Claiming credit

When you have completed this element you will need to write in your record book or folder *how, when, where* and *what* you have done to prove that you are competent.

The following is an example of how one trainee completed this claim.

2.1.a When I was on reception in the college training office for two days I answered the switchboard (BT 2+8) promptly. I said 'Good Morning/ Afternoon, Training Office. How may I help you?'

2.1.b I asked who was calling and how I could help them. I would take a message if a person was not available (see folder for evidence).

2.1.c I was always polite and courteous. If I could not help I would transfer the caller to someone who could, eg my supervisor (see log in folder).

2.1.d I was never asked to give confidential information, but if I had been asked to do so, I would have told my supervisor immediately.

2.1.e I used the *Phone Book* and *Yellow Pages* to find external numbers. I had to call these from the switchboard and then transfer the calls to an extension when connected. I announced the call before transferring it.

2.1.f I asked the purpose of all outgoing calls and the number required. I kept a log (see folder).

2.1.g I did not have any faults, but if I had any I would have reported these to my supervisor and then contacted BT on 154 to report the fault, if told to do so.

■ Element 2.2

RECEIVE AND RELAY ORAL AND WRITTEN MESSAGES

Communication skills include the ability to take messages, record them accurately and ensure they are received by the correct person. A message is of no use if it is not received by the person for whom it was intended, or by an alternative person who can deal with it. All information received must be checked before passing it on, and must be communicated accurately or it will cause confusion and waste valuable time.

The information you receive will be presented in a variety of forms. You may receive oral (spoken) information, either face-to-face or perhaps over the telephone. This requires you to use listening skills so that nothing is misinterpreted. Written information may need to be checked and rewritten before it is communicated accurately, either in writing or orally, to the correct person or location.

It is essential that you are able to listen to and interpret information, use questions to check your understanding and seek additional information if required. Your ability to communicate information accurately, using the correct tone, style and vocabulary, will affect the way your colleagues and clients feel about you and the organisation for which you work.

In order for you to communicate efficiently, it is important that you are fully aware of the structure, location and responsibilities of people in your organisation. Each department will be responsible for different areas of work and there will be procedures for passing on information such as telephone messages and memorandums. When passing on written information the content must not only be accurate but also complete and grammatically correct. Poor spelling, grammar and incomplete information waste time and effort, and will not be tolerated for long by your work colleagues.

■ DIY 2.2.1

Obtain an organisation chart for your workplace or training centre. If there is not one available, draw it up yourself, indicating each department or person you deal with.

You receive the following telephone calls while working on the switchboard. What person or department in your organisation would deal with each call?

1. A request for a job application form
2. A request from the Health and Safety Officer to visit your premises
3. A member of staff wishes to check this week's wages

4 A stationery company sales representative
5 A magazine wants to know if you wish to advertise
6 A caller who wishes to make a complaint
7 The BT engineer, who is trying to locate your office
8 The VAT Inspector, wishing to make an appointment
9 A local college student looking for a work placement
10 The local police, making enquiries about a member of staff

During your working day you will be required to answer many incoming calls, or perhaps deal with callers face-to-face in a reception area. If the person required is not available you should offer to take a message. It is important that the message contains correct information and that you get all the key facts right.

Examples of key facts are:

- names
- dates
- times
- places
- purpose
- telephone/extension numbers

When passing on a message you do not have to write out the conversation word for word. You should identify the important parts and make sure these are checked with the caller – read back the message you have written for the caller to confirm that it is correct before he/she rings off or leaves.

DIY 2.2.2

You are working on the reception desk when a young lady walks in and asks to speak with Mr Bloom, the Accounts Manager. He is in a meeting all day and you explain that he will not be available until tomorrow morning. You ask if she would like to make an appointment with his secretary to see him. She explains that she already has an appointment to see him tomorrow at 9.00 am to discuss some outstanding bills. Her name is Kim West. She tells you that she owes the company money and has arranged to see Mr Bloom to try to find a way of paying off what she owes. However, she has been able to arrange an appointment with her bank manager at 9.00 am tomorrow instead. She thinks that, if she sees the bank manager first, she may be able to arrange a loan and then would not have to see Mr Bloom after all. The bank manager has asked that she arrange for Mr Bloom to telephone the bank in the morning with details of the exact amount she owes. The number is 0498 478974 and the bank manager's name is Mr Jamie Blakemore. You tell her that you will pass a message to Mr Bloom's secretary explaining what she has just told you. However, it would be a good idea if she could telephone this afternoon to confirm with Mr Bloom's secretary that he will be able to contact the bank manager tomorrow.

1 Write out a message slip for Mr Bloom, with a copy to his secretary, Sharon Mackett. Do you think the message should have 'urgent' written on it?
2 Make a list of all the questions you would have asked during this conversation in order to gain all the key facts.

▶ *How would you relay a message verbally?*

You will relay messages verbally, face-to-face, or over the telephone, or on a telephone answering machine. Always remain calm and make sure you relay all the information correctly. If you make a mistake, stop, pause and start again – it is essential that you do not give incorrect information. If you give information face-to-face, make sure the other person writes it down. If they are unable to do this, make sure you send a written confirmation of the information given verbally.

When using an answering machine speak slowly and clearly, but remember that you have a limited amount of time in which to deliver the message before the tape cuts off. State the most important part of the message first – your name and contact telephone number. Then give details of your enquiry. This means that if you do get cut off, you can still be contacted when the message is played back.

Modern answering machines will give details of the date and time the message was left. However, as a caller you will not know if you are speaking to a machine with this facility. You should, therefore, include in your message the date and time of your call. Imagine your office had been unattended on Monday and Tuesday and you have received the following messages upon your return:

> *'This is the BT Engineer to say that we shall be installing your new switchboard tomorrow.'*

What day do you think he means? It could be Tuesday or Wednesday!

> *'This is the plumber. I called earlier but no-one was there so I'll*

call again tomorrow one hour later than I did today to see if you are there.'

This one is even more difficult. There is no way of telling the day or time to which he is referring.

Leaving messages on an answering machine becomes easier with practice. You will learn with experience quickly to pick out the key points to be made when you are answered by a machine. When you hear the recorded message, do not automatically put the receiver down, as leaving a message will save you time in the long run and improve your own efficiency.

■ DIY 2.2.3

In DIY 2.2.2 you wrote a message on behalf of Kim West. Imagine you are Kim West and you have telephoned the organisation instead of calling in person. You are answered by the telephone answering machine and need to relay the information verbally. Use either a cassette recorder or answering machine to relay the key facts (using your own name instead of Kim's).

You and your supervisor will need to play back the message to check that you have communicated effectively using an appropriate tone, style and vocabulary. When you play back the message, write out a telephone message slip. Compare this with the key facts listed in DIY 2.2.2 to ensure that you have not omitted anything important.

Did you remember to give details of the date and time of your call?

► *How do you establish rapport and goodwill with colleagues and clients?*

This will come with experience as you get to know colleagues better and understand the role they play in the organisation. Some organisations will have an informal atmosphere with all personnel on first name terms; others will require a more formal approach where superiors are referred to as Mr— or Mrs— and so on. You may find that, while you are on first name terms with members of staff, they may still require you to be more formal when dealing with an outside visitor.

Customers and clients of an organisation should always be greeted and attended to politely and only be referred to by their first name if they are known by you very well. Do not fall into the trap of calling someone by their first name because they have introduced themselves as, for example, John Brown. Members of staff who are happy to be called by their first names in conversation may still require you to refer to them formally when in the presence of customers or when dealing with telephone enquiries.

When you are new to an organisation you will be unsure of how to address staff and clients. Never be over-familiar. It is better to be over-polite until such time as you are told to use first names. When dealing with others try to follow a few simple rules, such as:

- Sound business-like; do not use slang
- If someone has helped you, say thank you (they will be more likely to help again if you have been polite)
- When requesting anything, say please (people are more likely to respond)
- Get involved and show interest in what you and others are doing
- Be helpful; if you have nothing to do, ask if you can help someone else
- Use a person's name during conversation and ensure you introduce yourself
- Do not be afraid to ask for help or clarification if you are unsure of anything
- Listen to what is being said (do not be over-familiar and join in with conversations you know nothing about – listen and learn)
- Never discuss anything you have heard with other people (as a newcomer, you never know who you might be talking to)

■ DIY 2.2.4

Read through the following sentences and fill in the missing words.

formally	*happy*	*greeted*	*played*
politely	*name*	*tape*	*enquiry*
purpose	*limited*	*dates*	*key facts*
message	*checked*	*available*	*valuable*
confusion	*received*	*accurately*	*messages*

1 Communication skills include the ability to take _ _ _ _ _ _ _ _ _, record them _ _ _ _ _ _ _ _ _ _ _ and ensure they are _ _ _ _ _ _ _ _ _ by the correct person. All information received must be _ _ _ _ _ _ _ before passing it on, and it must be communicated accurately or it will cause _ _ _ _ _ _ _ _ _ _ and waste _ _ _ _ _ _ _ _ _ time.

2 If the person required is not _ _ _ _ _ _ _ _ _ _ you should offer to take a _ _ _ _ _ _ _ _. It is important that the message contains correct information and that you get all the _ _ _ _ _ _ _ _ right.

3 Examples of key facts are: names; _ _ _ _ _; times; places; _ _ _ _ _ _ _ _; telephone/extension numbers.

4 When using an answering machine, speak slowly and clearly, but remember that you have a _ _ _ _ _ _ _ _ amount of time in which to deliver the message before the _ _ _ _ cuts off. State the most important part of the message first – your _ _ _ _ and contact telephone number. Then give details of your _ _ _ _ _ _ _ _. This means that, if you do get cut off, you can still be contacted when the message is _ _ _ _ _ _ back.

5 Customers and clients of an organisation should always be _ _ _ _ _ _ _ _ and attended to _ _ _ _ _ _ _ _ _ and only be referred to by their first name if they are known by you very well. Members of staff who are _ _ _ _ _ to be called by their first names in conversation may still require you to refer to them _ _ _ _ _ _ _ _ _ when in the presence of customers or when dealing with telephone enquiries.

Completing Element 2.2

To complete this element on receiving and relaying oral and written messages, you will need to put all the DIY tasks in your work folder and carry out a final assessment. This assessment must cover receiving three consecutive messages on a minimum of four separate occasions. You will be able to use the assessments involving oral and written messages completed for Element 2.1 towards this. If you are responsible for taking and relaying messages at work, keep a log detailing what you do. Your supervisor can sign this log to be used as evidence for this element.

Claiming credit

When you have completed your final assessment, you will need to write in your record book or folder *how, when, where* and *what* you have done to prove that you are competent.

The following is an example of how one trainee completed this claim:

2.2.a During a 2-day period in the training centre administration office I received telephone and personal callers. I asked questions courteously and checked information with the caller.

2.2.b I noted telephone messages and messages left by personal callers on message slips and delivered these immediately to the right person or department.

2.2.c I always checked information was correct by repeating it to the caller. If I left a message, I made sure it was accurate and contained all relevant points.

■ Element 2.3
SUPPLY INFORMATION FOR A SPECIFIC PURPOSE

Whichever type of work you do, you will at some time be asked for information. It is unlikely that you will be able to remember everything and it is important that you know where to find the information required. Your boss may ask, 'What is Joanne's room number?' or, 'What is the 'phone number for directory enquiries international?'

The type of question will vary, some will be easy to answer and others may take some time to research. The answers will need to be written down and fed back to the correct person.

▶ *What sources of information are there?*

There are hundreds of sources of information, but the ones you are most likely to use could include:

- people, including friends and work colleagues
- newspapers and magazines
- telephone directories – internal (lists all the people in the company along with their room number, location and extension number), and external (such as local directories, *Yellow Pages*, *Thomson directories*)
- fax and telex directories, *Yellow Pages* and *Thomson directories*
- filing systems – paper-based, computerised and microfiche

- reference books and libraries
- organisations, eg AA, RAC, BT, Tourist Information Office, Local Council
- specialist organisations connected with your business
- company literature, eg organisation chart, price lists, sales leaflets, stock lists, staff handbooks
- viewdata, eg Teletext, Prestel and Ceefax.

DIY 2.3.1

Select five sources of information from the above list and find out exactly what information is supplied by them. List the types of information in the form of a chart, using the following headings. Some examples have been completed for you.

Information source	Information available	How it is accessed	How it is presented
Dictionary	Spellings and meanings of words and abbreviations Weights and measurements* Countries of the world* States of the USA*	Reading, visual	Written in a book
Directory enquiries	Telephone numbers and codes	Telephone verbal	Verbal, from the operator and tape recording
Teletext	Pages of information on holidays, goods for sale, TV programmes, weather, etc	TV	Written on screen

* Not in all dictionaries

The communication skills you need to develop in order to collect and supply information are: listening, verbal, writing and visual, and you also need common sense!

▶ *How should you use the skills?*

Listening skills. It is important to listen carefully to other people when they are passing information to you. The person may be speaking to you face-to-face, over the telephone (directly or from a recorded message), over an intercom or loudspeaker. Always have a pen and notepad ready in case you need to jot down information. Do not rely on remembering it correctly – especially if numbers are involved. If you are unsure of anything, and you are in direct contact with the other person, ask for it to be repeated and you may be able to ask further questions in order to get more explanation. Read back to the other person the notes you have made, to check that you have the correct information, especially any numbers involved. (These could be telephone numbers, prices, quantities, measurements, code numbers, etc). If the person has requested information from you make sure you fully understand what is needed before you answer. Do not give out false information or information you are unsure of – check it first.

■ DIY 2.3.2

Your manager, Mr Johnson, has asked you to plan a route for him to travel by car from Birmingham to Manchester. List the roads you would expect him to use and work out the mileage. He will be able to claim 30p for every mile travelled and will be going there and back in the same day. Supply him with the information in the form of a memo (see page 85 if you are unsure how to lay out a memo) and include the name of the information source which you use.

Verbal skills. How you request or pass on information is extremely important. If you are asking someone to help, or you are dealing with a customer or colleague, you should do this politely. Speak slowly so that the person can understand exactly what you are saying and does not get confused. If you have unusual words or names to pass on, spell them out, using a telephone alphabet (see below) if necessary. Some letters and numbers sound similar over the telephone, such as t, b, p, e, g and 5 and 9. If there is a lot of information it may be better to confirm it in writing later.

A Alfred
B Benjamin
C Charlie
D David
E Edward
F Frederick
G George
H Harry
I Isaac
J Jack
K King
L Lucy
M Mary
N Nellie
O Oliver
P Peter
Q Queen
R Robert
S Samuel
T Tommy
U Uncle
V Victor
W William
X X-ray
Y Yellow
Z Zebra

If you wanted to spell the words '*mot juste*' using the telephone alphabet, you would say M for Mary, O for Oliver, T for Tommy, new word J for Jack, U for Uncle, S for Samuel, T for Tommy and E for Edward.

■ DIY 2.3.3

Telephone or visit your local tourist information office and ask them for the name, address and price charged of two local places where you could get bed and breakfast accommodation.

Write down your information in the form of a note.

Writing skills. You may be asked to supply or to request information in writing. This may be in the form of a letter, memo, message form, report, notice, quotation, enquiry form, etc. If your writing is poor, you should try to print or type your documents. Ensure you check your spelling and grammar, especially when sending documents outside your organisation. The image you wish to present is of a well-organised, efficient person, which will also reflect on your company. Do not write down any unnecessary information, or it may lead to confusion. Make sure you select a suitable method of presenting the information. For instance, you should not send a memo to a customer or client as a memo is only used internally, within the organisation. Some types of information are better displayed as a chart or diagram.

■ DIY 2.3.4

The Sales Manager is going to Northamptonshire, and has asked you to find out what counties surround Northamptonshire. Make a sketch of the area and label the counties correctly.

Write at the bottom of your sketch the information source used.

Visual skills. You should try to be observant and notice things, as well as being able to find things. It can be embarrassing if someone asks you to collect an item from a particular place and you cannot see it! It may be that the item is not exactly where the person said it would be, but on the next shelf or in the next drawer. Look carefully and make sure you do not miss anything. Only when you have looked in all the possible places should you return and report that you cannot find the item. If you are able to notice things that need doing, you may be able to predict some of the requests from your customers or colleagues. This will make you a more efficient and valuable employee, and people will appreciate the work that you do, especially if it saves them time.

■ DIY 2.3.5

On the way home from college or work today, look to see how many information sources you can see. List these and write next to them the type of information being supplied.

Common sense. A person with common sense is worth a great deal to any company or organisation. Having common sense in dealing with everyday matters is very important. You should not act in an immature way, be careless or unwise. If you show that you can act in a responsible fashion and respond to requests correctly, you are likely to be given more responsibility with less supervision. In this way you will be able to make your job more interesting and look for promotion or a better job, once you are experienced. Those people who need constant supervision and are unable to work by using their initiative become a burden to the organisation. Try to see how you can help, inform, receive and pass on information, and anticipate the needs of others, without having to be asked every time.

■ DIY 2.3.6

How would you present the following information?

1 You have been asked by the office manager to get the train departure and arrival times for a trip to Brighton next week.

2 A customer wants to know the price, discounts, colours and delivery times of your range of patio furniture.

3 A colleague has asked you to find out which files are in the top drawer of the filing cabinet.

4 The receptionist wants to know what time you will be leaving work today.

5 The Personnel Manager has asked you to let the staff know about a dinner dance to be held in two months' time.

6 The Sales Manager wants the total sales for the month achieved by the six sales representatives of your company.

▶ *What about confidentiality?*

You must be sure that the information you are supplying is not confidential or, if it is, that you are supplying it to someone who is allowed to have it. You should check with your supervisor if you are unsure about a person's authority. For example, if you are requested by a telephone caller to supply the home address and telephone number of the sales manager, you should politely refuse and, if the caller insists, refer them to your supervisor. Confidential information may also include the financial and accounts details of the organisation, staff location and detailed timetables, security arrangements, customers' records and requirements. In every situation you need to find out who is requesting the information and whether they are entitled to have it. *Never* disclose to competitors information about your organisation which can be used to benefit them or be used against your organisation. This could include customer details, financial position or future plans.

■ DIY 2.3.7

Make out a chart with the following headings for your work folder:

Date	Information required	Source used	Method by which information passed on
10/6/9–	cinema times	local paper	verbally
12/6/9–	train times	telephoned local station	written note
18/6/9–	enrolment dates for College	called in to College	prospectus collected
20/6/9–	file requested	filing system	file passed on

Complete the record for two weeks (or until you have 20 entries), putting the date in the first column; the information you were asked to supply in the second column; the source you used to find the information in the third column; and the way in which you passed the information on to another person in the last column. This chart will become an important part of your evidence, so keep it up to date and clean.

When supplying information, apart from deciding on the source to use and the method of presentation, you must also take time into consideration. Some information will be required urgently and you may only have a few minutes in which to supply it; other information will take longer to find and you may need a day or more to find it. You should always be able to estimate the time you require to find the information and let the person know how long it will be before you return with the necessary facts. If there is going to be a delay and it will take longer than you thought, go back and tell the person, so that they do not think that you have forgotten about it.

If you have several requests, put them in a priority order, so that the most urgent and important ones are first. Set your own deadlines if you do not have to meet a particular time or date; otherwise you may find that things get left and forgotten. You may have other duties to carry out, such as dealing with the post, answering the telephone, running errands,or sorting out stock. You will need to include these duties in your priority list, especially when some have to be done at a particular time, eg sending the post or answering the telephone.

Completing Element 2.3

To complete this element on supplying information for a specific purpose, you will need to put all the DIY tasks in your work folder, and carry out a final assessment. This assessment must cover a minimum of six requests for information on three separate occasions and be within time constraints. The information provided must be presented in notes, letters, memos and verbally (at least one of each is recommended). If you are working and provide information to clients, customers or colleagues, you will be able to complete a table similar to that in DIY 2.3.7.

Claiming credit

Once you have completed your final assessment, you will need to write in your record book or folder *how, when, where* and *what* you have done to prove that you are competent.

The following is an example of how one trainee completed this claim.

2.3.a When carrying out my assignment I had to use the rail timetables, atlas, dictionary, Prestel, and library microfiche. I made sure I used the correct source for the information needed.

2.3.b I obtained the information required and made notes before presenting it.

2.3.c I provided the information to the person requesting it as quickly as possible. I set my own deadlines when none were set for me.

2.3.d I was unable to find the information requested and I told the person immediately. When I was unable to use the Prestel system I informed my tutor that there would be a delay of two days.

Element 2.4
DRAFT ROUTINE BUSINESS COMMUNICATIONS

As part of your duties in an office you will probably have to write letters and memos, or it could be that you have to draft a letter or memo for someone else's signature. Whether you are writing a business document for your own signature or someone else's, it is important to ensure that the information is correct and that your document is well prepared and presented using the correct layout. The correct layout will depend upon the rules of your organisation. If the organisation has an accepted 'house style' all employees will be expected to use the approved layout and there may be a guidance manual for you to follow.

Most draft documents are in double line spacing, which leaves room for someone to insert extra sentences or to write instructions on the document. You may be instructed to use a particular layout for a document or for all your work, which could be fully blocked (*see* page 84), semi-blocked, or indented. If you are unsure how to lay out a document, always ask for an example to follow.

The type of words and phrases you use in letters and memos should be simple and clear. Try to avoid sounding too familiar, indifferent or careless: be friendly and not hostile. The content of the document should be clear and not ambiguous or vague, which would only confuse the person receiving it. Do not waffle; keep to the point.

■ DIY 2.4.1

Write out the following sentences, leaving two or three blank lines underneath each one. Then rewrite the sentences using clearer English. If you do not understand any of the words, look them up in a dictionary.

1 Due to the proliferation of personnel utilising the establishment's stamps we will be procuring a franking machine.

2 As from the 3rd inst all solicitations for petty cash should be concluded by the 20th of every month.

3 I acknowledge receipt and thank you for your letter of the 2nd of last month and am pleased to be able duly to accord your requisition.

▶ *Identifying the parts of a business letter*

All business letters have a similar structure regardless of the content or nature of the letter. The paper used for business letters is usually preprinted with the organisation's name and address, telephone number (as well as fax or telex numbers if they have these) and the registered number (if the company is registered). The registered address and the names of the directors or partners should also be shown. Most of the letters you write will probably be in the blocked or semi-blocked layout. Fig 2.5 is an example of the layout for a semi-blocked letter and a description of the common parts. However, organisations will have their own approved 'house style' and it is important that you follow the approved layout when you are employed or during work experience.

Our reference
Your reference

Name
Address   Date

Postcode

Salutation

HEADING

Paragraph

Paragraph

Complimentary close
(Leave a minimum of 25mm here)
Writer's name
Designation or department

Encs(4)

Fig 2.5 An example of a semi-blocked letter

Our reference. This is an identity code which the writer can recognise. It may be a customer account number, file number, case number, the department name or the writer's and typist's initials, eg **LSB/PAG**.

Your reference. If the person writing to you has used a reference then you should include this when you reply.

Date. This is usually typed as **day month year**, eg **24 May 1994** without punctuation (in blocked or semi-blocked layout). It should be written on the right-hand side of the paper, opposite the name and address of the addressee, or on the left-hand side of the paper above the name and address of the addressee.

Name and address. The name and address of the person to whom you are writing (the addressee) should be at the left-hand side of the page, without punctuation. It should be written in the same way as you would write on an envelope.

Salutation. This starts Dear . . . . If you know the person to whom you are writing, eg Mrs Smith, Mr Johnson, then you would probably write: **Dear Mrs Smith** or **Dear Mr Johnson**. First names would be used instead if you know the person reasonably well, eg **Dear Mary**. Sometimes a supervisor may like to write the salutation of a typed letter by hand, as a personal touch. If you are unsure to whom the letter should be addressed, you may write: **Dear Sir/Madam.**

Heading. Any heading for the letter should be written at the left-hand margin, after the salutation and before the first paragraph of the letter starts. It can be in capitals or with initial capitals only and underlined.

Paragraphs. These will contain the details of the letter and you should have a blank line between each paragraph to show where the next one begins. Do not indent the paragraph; start it at the left-hand margin.

Complimentary close. This ends the letter. If **Dear Sir or Madam** has been used, then the close will be **Yours faithfully**. If the salutation was **Dear Mrs** —, **Dear Mr** — or **Dear Jenny,** then the close will be **Yours sincerely**. The complimentary close should be written about half-way across the page for a semi-blocked letter.

Writer's name. A space should be left after the complimentary close of about 25 mm (to allow the person to sign the letter). Below this space the writer's name should be typed or otherwise written in capitals, so that the receiver can easily read it, starting at exactly the same point across the paper as the complimentary close so it lines up under it.

Designation or Department. The writer's position is sometimes written directly underneath their name, eg Company Secretary, Departmental Supervisor. If the employees do not have special positions, then the department name may be used, eg Purchasing Department.

Enclosures. If you refer to any enclosures in the letter, then it is usual to show this at the bottom of the letter to make it noticeable. This reminds you to include the enclosures when putting the letter in the envelope and it also helps the person receiving it to check the contents are correct when opening the envelope. If there is only one Enclosure, the word **Enc** should be written at the left-hand margin about 2 spaces below the designation. If there is more than one enclosure, the word **Encs** should be written with the number of enclosures in brackets afterwards, eg **Encs (4)**. No full stop should be used on the abbreviation Enc or Encs.

Leave plenty of room for the writer to sign. Usually 4 to 5 lines is sufficient, but if your manager has a particularly large signature, more space may be required. A letter should only be signed by the person whose name appears in the signature block. If they are absent from the office and you are authorised to sign on their behalf the letters **pp** should be written by the writer's name and you should sign your own name in the space for the signature. The letters pp stand for *per pro,* which means 'for and on behalf of'. The receiver of the letter will then know that the writer was unable to sign.

If a letter is too long to fit on one page, it will be necessary to continue on to a second sheet. This continuation sheet should be plain paper, the same size and colour as the first sheet but without the preprinted name of the organisation. The margins used should be the same as on the first sheet and at the top of the page the name of the person you are writing to, the page number and the date should be written. Usually these would be placed below each other at the left-hand margin:

Mrs P Scott
2
31 December 199–

■ DIY 2.4.2

You are the Events Secretary for the Hensbury Institute and you are writing to one of the local politicians, Mr Adams, to ask him to present the prizes at your annual presentation evening on 20 May. Draft a suitable letter using the semi-blocked layout shown in Fig 2.5. Our reference is *Your initials*/PAG. The letter should be addressed to: Mr J Adams 23 Glenview Road Parkpole HENSBURY HB12 4JJ. Use today's date and the salutation: Dear Mr Adams. The heading for the letter should be: Presentation Evening. Ask Mr Adams if he will be able to present the prizes again this year and to make a short speech. The evening is due to begin at 7.30 pm and we would like Mr Adams to arrive at 7.00 pm if that is convenient to him. Sign the letter with your own name and use the designation Events Secretary. There will be no enclosures.

▶ *Special markings or instructions*

Sometimes your manager may ask you to put a special marking or instruction on the letter and on the envelope. It may be that the letter is CONFIDENTIAL, URGENT, PERSONAL, PRIVATE, FOR THE ATTENTION OF (a particular person), sometimes abbreviated to FAO. These special markings are written, in capitals, two lines above the name and address block and below the references. They should be written as the first line on the envelope. They are placed here so that anyone sorting the post will see the marking quickly and ensure that the appropriate action is taken. However, organisations may have their own house style and you should check this when you are working for them.

Unless your manager has instructed you otherwise, you should never open letters marked 'Personal', 'Private' or 'Confidential'. In some departments the majority of the letters received are marked 'Confidential' (such as personnel departments) and you should check with your immediate supervisor which letters you are authorised to open. The letters marked 'For the attention of' may be sorted in the usual way and opened on receipt in the department. Urgent letters should be delivered as quickly as possible, usually by hand as soon as they are received. These letters may be opened on receipt if they are not marked 'Personal', as urgent action may be required.

■ DIY 2.4.3

What action would you take if you received an envelope which had the following special markings?

Marking	**Action**
CONFIDENTIAL	
PRIVATE	
PERSONAL	
URGENT	
FOR THE ATTENTION OF THE BUYER	
URGENT AND PERSONAL	

▶ *Identifying the parts of a memorandum*

A memorandum is used to write to people within the same organisation. Some organisations will have preprinted paper especially for the purpose which may also include their logo or name.

The word MEMORANDUM is usually placed at the top of the paper, sometimes in spaced capitals. It may be centred or at the margin. Two lines below, will be the words To: and Date: and underneath From: and Ref:. One clear space is left between these items to allow for the details to be put beside each item. The reference is the same as for a letter, an identity code which the writer can recognise. For example, it may be a file number or the computer filename under which the document was saved.

MEMORANDUM	
To:	Date:
From:	Ref:

Fig 2.6 Heading for a memorandum

■ DIY 2.4.4

Write a memo to your manager, saying that you have a hospital appointment on the first Thursday of next month (find out the date from your calendar). The appointment is at 9.00 am and you should be back in the office by 11.00 am.

Most memos (or memorandums, the plural for memorandum) are not signed, but some writers prefer to initial the memo after the last paragraph, so that the person receiving it knows that the sender has read and approved it.

If enclosures are included with a memo, it is usual to type or write **Enc** or **Encs** below the last paragraph and against the left-hand margin, in the same place as for a letter.

Most memos are not posted in envelopes but can be circulated in the internal post, unless they are marked 'Confidential'. Some companies have special internal envelopes for circulating internal post and these would be used for memos.

The special markings used on letters may also be used on memos. If there is room the special marking would be typed or written underneath the word 'Memorandum' (and above To:). Quite often, however, there is not enough room here, so it may be written above the word 'Memorandum' or opposite, at the left-hand margin.

■ DIY 2.4.5

1 Write a memo from yourself to the Manager of the Southern Branch, confirming that your Manager, Miss Wells, will be attending their annual presentation on 1 May. Request that a car space be reserved for her. Use a suitable reference.

2 Write a memo from yourself to the Administration Manager, asking to be provided with up-to-date prices for the following goods: 2 four-drawer cabinets (beige colour); 12 filing trays; 486 PC double disk drive with colour monitor, keyboard and mouse. This is urgent as your Manager would like to purchase the items next week. Do not forget the special marking and use a suitable reference.

3 You work in the Personnel Department and have a new member of staff, Lisa Pickett, who has joined the Accounts Department. Your supervisor has asked you to make sure Lisa has settled in after the first week. During conversation you find out that she is new to the area and has been having difficulty in getting to work. Write a memo providing her with all the information regarding the local transport services, including telephone numbers of local stations and depots. She lives near you and would use the same bus route(s).

▶ *Spelling*

All business documents should be free from typing and spelling errors. If you know that your spelling is poor, it is even more important to make sure that you check your documents carefully. Use a dictionary to look up words of which you are unsure. Use the spellcheck facility on the word processor, but do not forget that a spellcheck will not find errors in grammar. Keep a list of words that you use frequently and misspell. Only by practising the correct spelling will you get it right. Any letter or memo that you send out with errors will give the receiver a poor impression of you and your department. It may even result in a loss of business, if people think your standards are low.

Completing Element 2.4

To complete this element on draft routine business communications, you will need to put all the DIY tasks in your work folder and carry out a final assessment. This assessment must cover drafting a minimum of two letters and two memos which include an enquiry, confirmation and supplying of information. The content of the documents should contain simple and factual material with words and figures included. The documents must be readable, submitted in one of the approved formats ie blocked or semi-blocked or indented layout, and completed by a set deadline.

Claiming credit

Once you have completed your final assessment, you will need to write in your record book or folder *how, when, where* and *what* you have done to prove that you are competent. The following example shows how one trainee completed this claim.

2.4.a During my classwork and assignment I drafted two letters and two memorandums within the time limit set. I had to find out information to put into the documents, and I did this in the library.

2.4.b I handwrote and used the fully-blocked layout to present my draft documents. I used double line spacing to allow for alterations to be made.

UNIT 3
Data processing

■ Element 3.1

PRODUCE ALPHA/NUMERICAL INFORMATION IN TYPEWRITTEN FORM

To be able to complete this unit it will be necessary for you to type using a typewriter or word processor. Most books refer to the keyboard as a 'qwerty' keyboard. This just means that the keyboard has the keys in a particular order ie the top row, left-hand side is in the order of q w e r t y. No doubt you have received training on how to use the 'home keys' (the middle row of the keyboard) and all the other keys with the correct finger. It is important that you follow the instructions given by your tutor or given in the manual from which you have been learning.

All skills will improve with practice, whether you are roller skating, ten pin bowling, throwing darts or keyboarding. Keyboarding, in particular, will improve by continually using the correct finger for the correct key. Look at the document from which you are typing, not at your keyboard or hands while you type, and practise frequently. Thirty minutes every day for practice is better than three hours in one day, as it is the continuous practice that improves the skill.

▶ *Looking after your machine*

Your machine is like any other piece of equipment in that it needs looking after if you want it to work properly. The biggest problem in the office, as far as electrical equipment is concerned, is the amount of dust which they attract. Machines that are not regularly cleaned will collect dust and you will find that this will start to clog the machine, in the end it may stop. To avoid this happening, make sure that you cover the equipment at the end of each day with a dust cover.

You will find that the machines will gather dust on the outer casing, keyboard and screen (if there is one), and once a week these should be cleaned. *Remember – never clean a machine while it is connected to the mains electricity.*

Your college or organisation may have a special contract for machine cleaning, in which case they may not wish you to get involved with cleaning at all. Alternatively, someone in the organisation may be responsible for machine maintenance and cleaning. However, you should be aware of which parts may be cleaned and how to look after a machine of your own. The purpose of looking after the machine is to ensure that you reduce the chances of breakdown. All machines are supplied with manuals, and you should refer to these for precise instructions on how to look after your particular machine.

A special cleanser can be used to clean the outer casing (you will find some recommended brands in office equipment catalogues) but *do not* spray any electrical parts. Brushes or small vacuum cleaners can be used to clean away dust that has gathered in the keyboard or inside the case of typewriters. *Never* remove the case of a word processor or computer as there are parts in the machine which contain high voltage electricity.

▶ *Which parts can be cleaned on manual typewriters?*

These machines have mechanical parts and do not use electricity. When you press the key, it moves a bar, which makes the key come up from its place in the 'basket' of keys and hit the roller (the platen). As the key returns to its place, the carriage moves along one space. The front cover can be taken off the machine and a brush used to clear away the dust that has gathered. You may also find that there is a collection of rubber dust or correction paper dust that has collected under the typing point – all this can be brushed out.

If the machine is using a nylon ribbon, the keys may become blocked with ink. A small, hard-headed brush, like a toothbrush, needs to be used to remove the ink from the keys, especially keys such as o, a, e and p, as the ink collects inside the letters. A special type of cleaning paper (which is rough like a sandpaper) can be purchased to put in the machine. If you type all the letters of the alphabet (capitals and small letters, numbers and punctuation), the paper will automatically clean the keys. Although you may find that keys for o, a, e, p, etc need to be pressed more than once.

When you have finished cleaning the keys, always put some scrap paper in the machine and use all the keys again. This will make sure that any loose bits of ink and dirt are cleared away and do not make a mess on the next piece of typing you produce. If there is any dried correcting fluid on the machine, this should be carefully removed using a small piece of cotton wool and surgical spirit thinners or similar liquid. Make sure you replace the lid of the spirit after use, and store it safely in the storage cupboard.

Ribbons should be changed when required, but when cleaning the machine it is a good idea just to check that any nylon ribbon is still in order and that no holes are appearing near either of the spools.

The roller, or platen, on the machine is the large black roller that the paper feeds around. This must be kept smooth; otherwise, when the keys strike the paper, the letters will not form properly and will appear to be twisted. To help in preventing a platen from becoming damaged, always use a backing sheet with single sheets of paper. *Never* type without paper in the machine; otherwise, the keys will dig into the roller and cause permanent damage.

If you need to move the machine, first make sure that you lock the two margins together to stop the carriage from slipping while the machine is being lifted. The heaviest part of the machine, the back, should be nearest to you. If you are lifting from the floor, remember to bend your knees and keep your back straight – don't bend over. A trolley should be used whenever possible to move machinery.

▶ *Which parts of an electric or electronic machine can be cleaned?*

The difference between an electric and electronic machine is that the electronic machine contains microchips. Both machines do the same kind of work, but the electronic machine normally has more functions than the electric.

Unplug the machine from the mains electricity and then it can be cleaned on the outside, in the same way as a manual machine. Use a soft cloth and a recommended cleanser to remove the dirt, dust and correction fluid. *Do not* get any cleanser on the inner parts of the machine. On removing the front cover, the dust can be removed carefully from the inside. Use a soft brush to sweep the dust through the holes in the bottom of the machine's frame, or use a small hand-held vacuum cleaner.

If the printing head is a daisywheel or golf ball, and a nylon ribbon has been used, careful cleaning is necessary to remove bits of ink. Special fluid is available to soak the daisywheel and a brush can be used on the golf ball. Alternatively, both can be cleaned by using the correction sheet described in the section on cleaning manual machines.

All food and liquids should be kept well away from electrical equipment and, if an accident should occur, unplug the machine quickly to disconnect the equipment immediately from the electricity supply. Wet keyboards should be drained as quickly as possible and placed in a warm position to dry. Consult an expert before reconnecting the machine to the electricity supply, to make sure it is safe to do so. Any sticky liquids need to be cleaned off immediately.

Some machines have lights that flash or a beep that sounds when a fault occurs or a ribbon needs replacing. Look at the manual and ensure you are familiar with your machine so that you can identify faults when they occur.

▶ *Which parts of a word processor or computer can be cleaned?*

Very few parts can be cleaned without unplugging from the electricity supply. You should clean the screen regularly with an anti-static spray (recommended by the suppliers or local stationers). The casing can also be wiped clear of dirty fingermarks and dust. You will need to use a brush or small vacuum to remove dust from between the keys. *Never* remove the casing from computers or word processors. The screen of the monitor is sensitive and should not be left on when not in use, and static from the screen will also attract dust. If the machine is not going to be used for a while, turn the screen brightness down or turn the monitor off.

Keep food and liquids away from all WP and computer equipment. If an accident should occur, remove any disks, unplug immediately to disconnect the equipment from the mains electricity supply, and call your supervisor.

Fig 3.1 A computer system with printer

▶ *Printers*

If you have a word processor, it will be connected to a printer. There are two different types of printer, one called impact (where contact is made with the paper) and the other called non-impact (where contact is not made with the paper). Examples of impact printers are dot matrix printers or daisywheel printers.

A dot matrix printer creates the letters and other characters by printing dots in the shapes of the character. The more dots, the better the quality of the printing, as there is less space between the dots. The printer head is rectangular in shape and is made up of pin heads, the pins being pushed forward to form the shape of the character. Dot matrix printers can print 100–200 characters per second in draft form and can also produce diagrams and graphics.

A daisywheel printer works in a similar way to the daisywheel on a typewriter. The spokes of the printing wheel have characters on the end and the wheel turns to allow the correct character to touch the paper. A daisywheel can print up to 70 characters per second, but cannot produce diagrams and graphics.

Both of these types of printer are widely used, and if you have a computer at home with a printer, it is likely to be one of these. They are fairly inexpensive to buy but are fairly noisy and because of this they tend not to be used very much in large offices. To reduce the

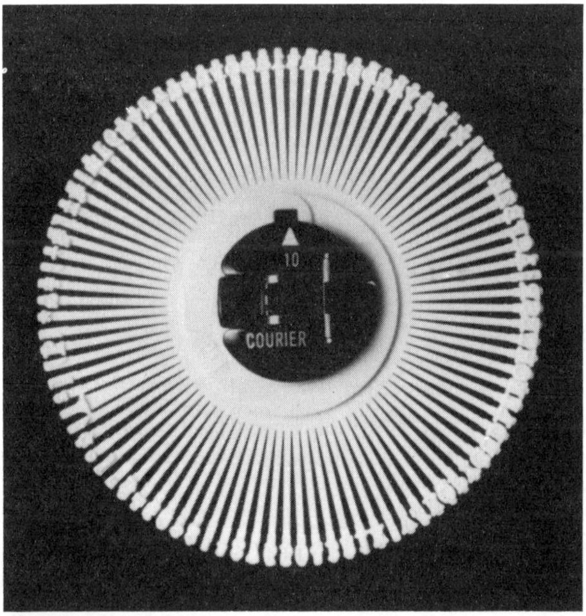

Fig 3.2 A daisywheel

noise, some companies cover the printer with an acoustic hood or screen, or when possible the printer may be located in a separate room.

Examples of non-impact printers are ink jet or laser printers.

An ink jet printer squirts tiny jets of ink on to the paper to form the characters, and the quality is very good. An ink jet printer can print up to five pages a minute. It is also able to form pictures and graphics.

A laser printer uses laser beams to transfer the characters from the screen on to a drum, which turns and transfers the characters on to the paper. Lasers can produce a page of A4 typing in about six seconds. They can also produce excellent graphics (graphs, diagrams and pictures).

Ink jet and laser printers are quiet to run but are more expensive than the impact printers to buy. The maintenance of the laser printers can also be quite expensive as they require toner and parts to be changed when high numbers of copies are made. Colour printing is possible but the print quality obtained may not be good enough for business letters.

► *What precautions should you take with computer equipment in the office?*

- Switch off all machinery at the end of the day. (The only exceptions may be the telephone answering machine, which will take telephone calls in your absence, and the fax machine, which may send and receive messages during the night.)
- Make sure that any connecting wires are not trailing across the floor. They should be secured under the desk or placed along the walls of the room.
- Do not overload sockets, Multi-extension leads should be used when several items need to be plugged in at the same time. Alternatively, extra sockets should be installed. Check the leads regularly for fraying or broken connections.

New regulations under the Health and Safety at Work Act 1974 (HASAWA) and the Electricity at Work Act (see page 215) state that all electrical equipment must be regularly checked to confirm it is safe to use. Consult your tutor or health and safety representative if you are not sure about the state of any of the equipment you use.

■ DIY 3.1.1

Find out the procedures to follow in your organisation or college in these following situations:

1. Your word processor will not load the program.
2. Your typewriter ribbon needs replacing.
3. You spill cola on your electronic typewriter keyboard.
4. A key comes off the keyboard of your computer.
5. You need some spray to clean your machines.

► *What is good posture?*

To make certain you do not suffer from strain and injury, you should sit in the most comfortable position for typing. Strain can occur to the neck, back, arms and legs, and can lead to serious complaints. To reduce the risk of RSI (repetitive strain injury), you should use a chair which can be adjusted to suit you. It should allow you to sit with your feet flat on the floor (use a footrest if necessary), and have an

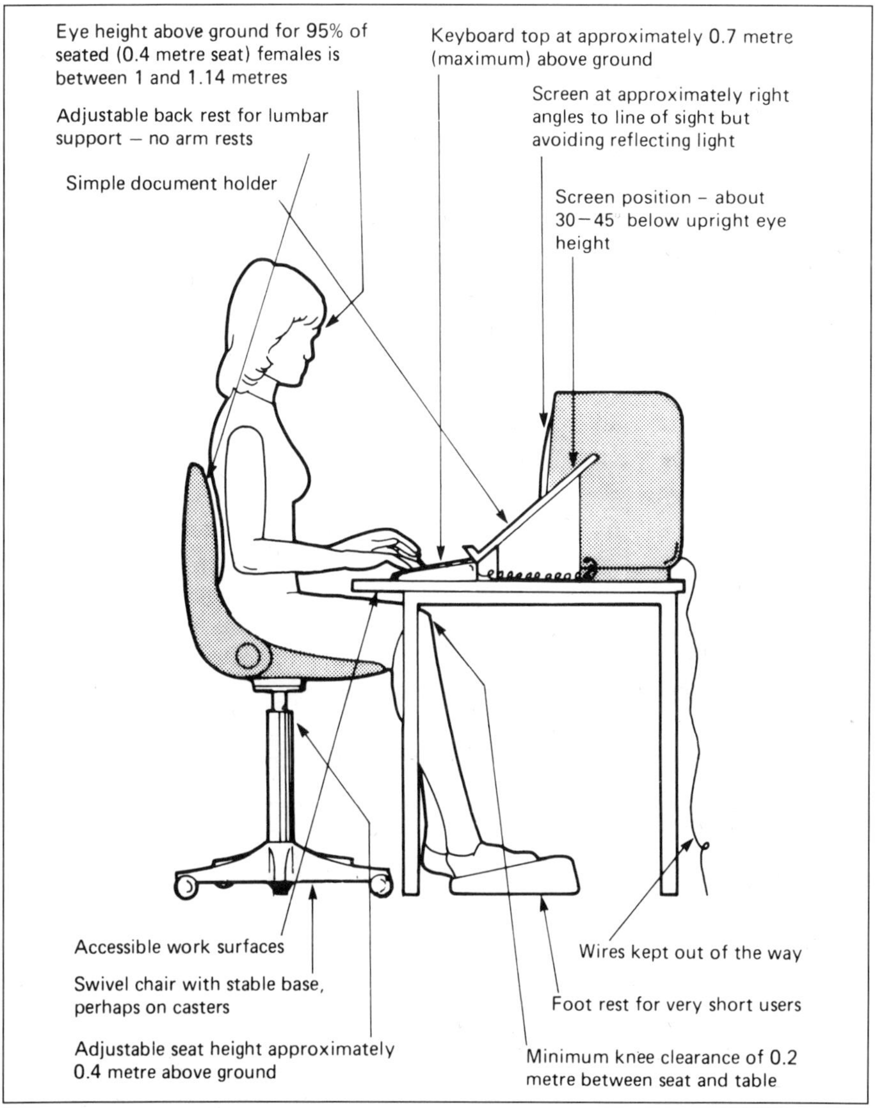

Fig 3.3 Good posture (taken from Association of Professional, Executive, Clerical and Computer Staff (APEX) Report of Office Technology Working Party)

adjustable backrest to support your lower back. Desks for typing are generally lower than normal desks, to allow for the keyboard to sit at the correct height.

Your head should be upright, otherwise you will find your neck will ache from constantly looking down at the desk. This means that the document you are copying from should be placed on a document holder, either to the right or left of your keyboard, whichever you find most comfortable.

▶ *Carrying out instructions*

Usually you will be given written documents or corrected typed documents to copy from, but occasionally someone may add a verbal instruction when they are handing you the work. Make sure that you write down any verbal instructions, either on your notepad or on the document itself. Remember to include such instructions when you carry out the work. An example might be, 'Oh, could you do that in double line spacing for me – thanks.', or, 'Would you do three copies when you type this please?'. Verbal instructions are just as important as written instructions, but are easier to forget or overlook if you are not careful.

Instructions may also be given about the size of paper to use. Letters are normally typed on A4 headed (printed with the organisation's name, etc) paper, although some companies use A5 headed paper. Memos, on the other hand, are commonly available in both A4 and A5 sizes. A4 portrait paper is 210 mm x 297mm, and has 100 spaces across the top and 70 lines down (assuming you are using elite type, which is 12 characters to 25 mm). A5 paper is exactly half this size, and A5 landscape has 100 spaces across the top and 35 lines down.

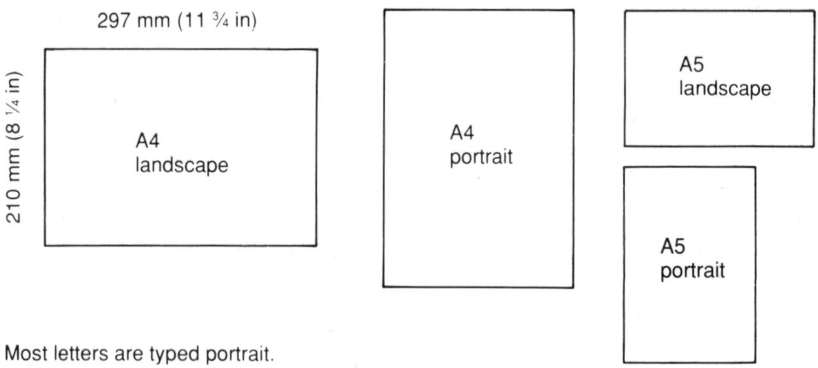

Fig 3.4 Paper sizes

The paper can be used either way: if the smaller side is put into the machine first, this is portrait (as you would draw a person's face); if the longer side is put in first, this is landscape (as you would draw hills or a view).

The most commonly used envelopes are the C5 (229 mm x 162 mm), which takes A5 paper unfolded or A4 paper folded once; C6 (162 mm x 114 mm), which takes A5 paper folded once, or A4 paper folded in half twice; and DL (220 mm x 110 mm) which takes A5 paper folded once or A4 paper folded into three (see page 168).

■ DIY 3.1.2

On a piece of A4 and A5 paper write or type the number of lines and spaces available on each, showing which way is landscape and which is portrait. Fold three pieces of A4 paper into the three most common envelope shapes and write the correct number on each.

If you have already completed the Unit 6, DIY 6.2.3 task, you will not have to do this. Make a cross-reference note of this and insert it in your folder under Unit 3 as evidence. Your note should state: 'Evidence of my understanding of paper sizes, envelope sizes and uses is filed under Unit 6. DIY 6.2.3 task has been carried out.'

▶ *What are correction signs?*

People working in offices have not always received the correct training regarding layout of letters, memos and other documents. When they make corrections to documents they do not always use the approved correction signs. You will get to know each individual's peculiar signs, but if you are unsure at first, always ask. The accepted standard signs should be included as part of your training, and you should always use them yourself when correcting work.

■ DIY 3.1.3

Type out the meanings below and write the correction signs at the side (if you are not familiar with them, use any beginner's typewriting/keyboarding book for reference).

Meaning	Sign used in the margin	Sign used in the text
new paragraph		
insert full stop		
capital letter		
small letter		
no new paragraph		
insert space		
take out/delete		
close up space		
transpose (swap round)		
stet (leave as it was)		

Now type out the following paragraph as it is shown and then write the instructions for your typist to follow, making sure the correct signs are used:

> It was found, Upon looking at the glass closer, that there had been a forced entry.The wood had splnitered, and there were paint chippings on the floor. there could be no doubt about it now The police would have to be called.

(You will need to indicate: small letter, insert space, transpose, close up space, capital letter, and insert full stop.)

▶ *What are abbreviations?*

As well as using correction signs, you will probably find that people also use a variety of abbreviations. These could include:

ack	acknowledge	ref	reference
ackd	acknowledged	sec	secretary
amt	amount	sins	sincerely
amts	amounts	sh	shall
chq	cheque	shd	should
co	company	tel	telephone
del	delivery	th	thalt
dept	department	tog	together
ff	faithfully	wd	would
fr	from	wk	week
hv	have	wh	which
mth	month	wl	will
recd	received	yr	your or year (*the content of the sentence should tell you which one to use*)
rect	receipt		

See if you can make sense of this instruction:

> Wd you please send a rect to ref 134 and ack the order and chq, then tel and speak to the sec tell her we wl send the next del tog with the outstanding amts fr last wk.

The number of abbreviations in the above paragraph is obviously exaggerated, but people will often use abbreviations when drafting out letters, memos and reports for typing. You should always type the word in full. Never type words that you do not know – look them up in a dictionary and, if you cannot find them, ask. Quite often inexperienced staff will type absolute rubbish, thinking these are words they do not know. You will soon get to know the range of words used by your colleagues, and then you will be able to increase your speed and accuracy.

▶ *What type of layout should you use?*

As well as making sure the content of your work is correct, you will need to ensure the correct layout is used. Most organisations use a 'house style' that is a particular style which the organisation (the house) has approved and wishes all staff to use. An approved house style is used so that customers receive the same style of documentation, regardless of which department sends it. The documentation becomes part of the organisation's image and, if customers receive documents with mistakes left uncorrected, they will not get a very good impression of the organisation and may look elsewhere to do business in the future. Some organisations are extremely fussy about their house style, even stating what size of print and style to use.

You may have covered different types of layout as part of your training. The most commonly used is the fully-blocked layout for letters and memos, without punctuation (except in the paragraphs of the letter). In this style everything starts at the left-hand margin, usually 25mm from the edge of the paper. It is the quickest style to type, as you do not need to work out spacing, and it is the easiest to remember.

The date should always be written the same way, the most common order being day month year (without punctuation), eg 25 May 1994, whether it is typed at the top of the letter or in one of the paragraphs.

```
Reference

Date

Name
Address
Town
County
Postcode

Dear xxxxxxxx

HEADING (if there is one)

Paragraph xxxxxxxxxxxxxxxxxxxxxxxxxxxxxxxxxxx
xxxxxxxxxxxxxxxxxxxxxxxxxxxxxxxxxxxxxxxxxxxxx
xxxxxxxxxxxxxxxxxxxxxxxxxxxxxxxxxxxxxxxxxxxxx
xxxxxxxxxxxxxxx

Paragraph xxxxxxxxxxxxxxxxxxxxxxxxxxxxxxxxxxx
xxxxxxxxxxxxxxxxxxxxxxxxxxxxxxxxxxxxxxxxxxxxx
xxxxxxxxxxxxxxxxxxxxxxxxxxxxxxxxxxxxxxxxxxxxx
xxxxxxxxxxxxxxxxxxxxxxxxxxxxxxxx

Yours xxxxxxxx



Name
Department

Enc
```

Fig 3.5 Layout for a fully-blocked letter

```
MEMORANDUM

To

From

Date

Ref

HEADING (if there is one)

Paragraph xxxxxxxxxxxxxxxxxxxxxxxxxxxxxxxxxxxx
xxxxxxxxxxxxxxxxxxxxxxxxxxxxxxxxxxxxxxxxxxxxxx
xxxxxxxxxxxxxxxxxxxxxxxxxxxxxxx

Paragraph xxxxxxxxxxxxxxxxxxxxxxxxxxxxxxxxxxxx
xxxxxxxxxxxxxxxxxxxxxxxxxxxxxxxxxxxxxxxxxxxxxx
xxxxxxxxxxxxxxxxxxxxxxxxxxxxxxxxxxxxxxxx
```

Fig 3.6 Layout for a fully-blocked memo

The other layout style frequently used is the semi-blocked style. In this style the date is placed on the right-hand side of the letter or memo, and the signature block is centred (see Fig 3.7). The rest of the letter starts at the left-hand margin.

For memos typed in a semi-blocked layout the word 'memorandum' would be moved to the centre and the date and reference across to the left-hand side (see Fig 3.8).

Reference

Name
Address
Town
County
Postcode — Date

Dear xxxxxxx

HEADING *(if there is one)*

Paragraph xxxxxxxxxxxxxxxxxxxxxxxxxxxxxxxxxx
xxxxxxxxxxxxxxxxxxxxxxxxxxxxxxxxxxxxxxxxxxxx
xxxxxxxxxxxxxxxxxxxxxxxxxxxxxxxxxxxxxxxxxxxx

Paragraph xxxxxxxxxxxxxxxxxxxxxxxxxxxxxxxxxx
xxxxxxxxxxxxxxxxxxxxxxxxxxxxxxxxxxxxxxxxxxxx
xxxxxxxxxxxxxxxxxxxxxxxxxxxxxxxxxxxxxxxxxxxx
xxxxxxxxxxxxxxxxxxxxxxxxxxxxxxx

Yours xxxxxxxxxxx

Name
Department

Enc

Fig 3.7 Layout for a semi-blocked letter

```
                    MEMORANDUM

To                                       Date

From                                     Ref

HEADING (if there is one)

Paragraph xxxxxxxxxxxxxxxxxxxxxxxxxxxxxxxxxxx
xxxxxxxxxxxxxxxxxxxxxxxxxxxxxxxxxxxxxxxxxxxxx
xxxxxxxxxxxxxxxxxxxxxxxxxxxxxxxxx

Paragraph xxxxxxxxxxxxxxxxxxxxxxxxxxxxxxxxxxx
xxxxxxxxxxxxxxxxxxxxxxxxxxxxxxxxxxxxxxxxxxxxx
xxxxxxxxxxxx
```

Fig 3.8 Layout for a semi-blocked memo

When starting a new job, it is your responsibility to find out the style required for documents. Do not rely upon your existing knowledge, training and experience received at college or at previous companies. Some organisations will produce a manual or guide for staff to ensure that they follow the agreed layout for all documentation. If yours does not, ask for examples of past documents so you can copy their layout.

▶ *Guidelines for typing envelopes*

The guidelines for typing envelopes are given by the Post Office and suit the machinery installed to sort letters.

1 Type the address along the longer side of the envelope
2 The first line of the address should start at about one-third of the way across the envelope and half-way down
3 Each line of the address should have a separate line
4 The post town should be in capital letters
5 The postcode should be the last line, in capitals, on its own and with one space between the two parts, eg GN3 2NN

Mr J L Protheroe
Mobley & Co Ltd
1 Somerly Close
COVENTRY
CV3 2LA

Fig 3.9 Layout for an envelope

If there are any special instructions, such as URGENT, CONFIDENTIAL, For the attention of ..., these should be typed two lines above the name and address.

■ DIY 3.1.4

Type the following letter, using fully-blocked layout, and dating it for today. Also prepare an envelope and mark it CONFIDENTIAL. (If you do not have an envelope, fold a piece of A5 paper in half and type on one side.)

Mr J Bennett 24 Cottage Lane New Brocken YELVETIN YL3 4JJ

Dear Mr Bennett Thank you for your enquiry about our duck down pillows. We would be pleased to supply you with the Class A pillow at a price of £7.50 each. If you order more than 100 there will be a discount of 10% allowed. We can deliver within 7 days of receiving your order.

Please let us know if there is any further information you require. We look forward to hearing from you in the near future.

Yours sincerely J D FARMER Sales Department

▶ *Layout and presentation*

It may be left to you to decide how to lay out your documents and you will need to ensure that you select the most suitable method for the document concerned. As said before, layout is important because it reflects an image of the business. The most important rule is to be consistent. If you decide to leave two lines between each paragraph in a report, you should not suddenly start leaving three lines. Always look at previously typed documents to see how other staff have laid out the document or ask guidance from your supervisor.

▶ *What happens if you make mistakes?*

Everyone makes mistakes; the skill is in knowing when you make a mistake and correcting it so that no-one else knows! There is nothing worse than completing a letter or memo, and passing it to your manager to be signed, only to find it comes back with a big circle round a silly typing mistake. If you are using a typewriter, the whole document may have to be retyped.

It is most important to read everything you type before you hand it to the person for signature. You may believe that you 'know' when you have made a typing error, and realise an error has been made at the time, but there could still be some that you have not noticed. If you check your work carefully and produce accurate work, then your value to the organisation will increase. Most employers prefer someone who is accurate rather than fast. Proof-reading is a skill in the same way as typing and, the more you read, the quicker you will become at identifying errors.

▶ *What is proof-reading?*

This is when you read the document (proof) to ensure that it is correct in content and layout. Most people find proof-reading boring and it probably is, but it is an essential part of document production. It is useful to get someone else to read an important document for you, as they will be unfamiliar with the content, will concentrate more and it is likely they will find errors that you may have overlooked. It is common to find that when you are familiar with the document, you end up reading what should be there instead of what is actually there. Of course, someone else can only read the document, if it is not confidential. If you are unsure of how a word is spelt, look it up in a dictionary and keep a list of commonly misspelt words to refer to. If you have a word processor, it may have a spellcheck, in which case make sure you use this. However, you will still need to proof-read, as the spellcheck will not find grammatical errors or words that are incorrect, eg 'it' instead of 'is'; or incorrect punctuation, eg a full stop instead of a comma; or words, sentences or paragraphs that have been missed out completely; or words that have been typed twice, eg 'and and'. (Some spellchecks can, however, identify double words.)

■ DIY 3.1.5

Read the following paragraph and identify the 10 errors:

> As part of her work in personal, Jane had overalle responsibility for staff welfare and social activitys. In this capacity she is overseing the organisatoin of a a staff outing to the Isle of Wight which will take place on the second Wensday of next month. It will be lead by Janine Gordon, Chair of the Staff Social Comittee. A total of 45 staff have indicated there interest in attending.

How many of these errors would a spellcheck have missed?

▶ *What is the best method of correcting errors?*

It depends on the type of error and the type of equipment you are using. Obviously, you cannot use correction fluid for an error on a word processor screen! A corrected error should be unobtrusive, which means you should not be able to notice it. If you are using a typewriter you can use correction paper, where you place the paper over the error, type the error again and the error then has a white chalk covering which will allow you to type the correct character over the top of it. This method is unobtrusive, as long as you have the character lined up correctly otherwise the chalk covering misses part of the character and leaves that part uncorrected. However, this method should not be used for major errors, such as changing two sentences around, or taking out a whole sentence.

The other commonly-used method of covering errors is correcting fluid. There are two types on the market, water based and spirit based – both are equally good to use. Paint over the error with the fluid, wait until this is dry, and then type the correct character(s) over the paint.

■ DIY 3.1.6

In your own words, complete the following sentences. Try to write as much as possible to show you understand everything that has been covered so far.

1 Manual typewriters can be cleaned with ...

2 The two different types of ribbon used on typewriters are ...
3 The two different types of printer are ... and ..., and one example of each type is ... and ...
4 Strain can occur from bad posture of the neck, the ..., ... and ..., and to reduce the risk ...
5 House style is ...

Many electric and electronic typewriters have correction facilities on them. The correction tapes will either be similar to correction paper or coated on one side with a sticky substance. The type of correction tape used will depend on the type of ribbon used. Nylon ribbons use correction paper, and carbon ribbons use lift-off correction tape. It is called lift-off tape as this is exactly what it does, lifting the error from the paper. If you look at the correction tape when you replace it you will see the carbon characters are stuck to it.

The disadvantage with this method of correction is that it leaves an indentation in the paper, and the better the quality of the paper, the more obvious the indentation. This is not a problem if another character is to be typed on top, but if it is between two words or at the end of a sentence, the indentation may be noticeable. Some people may object to sending out a document with noticeable indentations.

Some electronic machines also have a line display, which allows you to correct words or sentences before you actually print them.

When major errors occur in typewritten documents it may be possible to retype the one page necessary or to 'cut and paste'. This means that the correct paragraphs are cut out and glued in the correct order around the newly-typed paragraphs. The whole document is then photocopied before being passed to your manager. This method cannot be used for letters and it may be unsuitable for some occasions, as for instance when your boss wants the original to be sent.

If you do use a word processor, make sure that you proof-read on screen properly, otherwise sheets of paper and time are wasted unnecessarily in printing work that is full of errors. The main advantage, though, is that errors corrected in this way will not appear at all on the printed document.

■ DIY 3.1.7

Type the following passage within 10 minutes, using any method of correcting your errors as long as it is unobtrusive. Remember to proof-read.

Modern technology has seen the development of many different electronic methods for the sending and receiving of information. Digital technology in the form of computer chips and fibre optics, together with the increased use of communications satellites, can now allow direct transmission of data at great speed, whether locally, nationally or worldwide.

The most recent advances have seen the introduction to offices of 4 main facilities – electronic paging, facsimile, telex and electronic mail. This equipment is offered in a competitive market by at least 2 telecommunications companies, who quote competitive rates for their equipment and services. A factor that will need to be taken into account when a company is planning to invest in new equipment.

Pagers are used by personnel who move around and so cannot always be contacted in their office. Pagers can be used internally (within the same building) or externally (throughout the local or national area).

This passage totals 150 words and you will need to type it in the 10 minutes allowed and have less than two errors in order to be able to pass your assessment.

Completing Element 3.1

To complete this element on producing documents you will need to put all DIY tasks in your folder and carry out a final assessment. This assessment must include the production of at least two letters or two memos (which have numbers included in the 150 words of text) and two envelopes. Different documents should be produced on three separate occasions within 10 minutes, and with less than two errors overall. Do not forget that any corrections made must be unobtrusive, and you should not miss out any of the numbers or have any error in the numbers. All the documents produced must be placed in your folder for the assessor and verifier to see.

Claiming credit

Once you have completed your final assessment, you will need to write in your record book or folder *how, when, where* and *what* you have done to prove that you are competent. If you hold a typewriting certificate you may be able to claim credit, so discuss this with your tutor.

The following is an example of how one trainee completed the claim.

3.1.a In class I have produced several letters, memos and envelopes that contain a minimum of 150 words and which include figures. These were typed in less than 10 minutes and contained two or less errors each time.

3.1.b I made unnoticeable corrections by using correction fluid and made sure it was dry before typing over it. When using the word processor, corrections were made on screen before printing.

3.1.c At no time did I show the work to other people (apart from my tutor). I kept it out of sight in my folder.

3.1.d The faults which occurred during the term were: the ribbon ran out, the printer jammed, and a program did not load. These were all reported to the tutor and, if not fixed, were written on the repair sheet.

Element 3.2

IDENTIFY AND MARK ERRORS ON SCRIPTED MATERIAL, FOR CORRECTION

If you are working as a general assistant, it may be that you send documents to the typing pool or clerk typist for typing. When they are returned to you for signature you must check thoroughly before signing and sending them out. We have already covered the skill of proof-reading as part of the last element and the use of correction signs. You should check spelling (look up any words you are not sure of), grammar, punctuation and content. Ensure that you use the approved correction signs whenever possible as this will make the typist's job easier and you will reduce the possibility of misunderstanding.

DIY 3.2.1

Words are often confused and misused. Write a sentence which uses the following similar words. Look up the words in a dictionary if you are not sure of their meaning. If you prefer, you can write two sentences. The first one has been done for you.

accept and *except*:

I accept your invitation for Monday and I will bring all the family, except for John.

check and *cheque*
advise and *advice*
compliment and *complement*
ensure and *insure*
quiet and *quite*
stationery and *stationary*
principle and *principal*

In addition to receiving documents from the typist you may also have to check computer printouts, handwritten material and numerical data. Apart from checking that the content and facts are correct, you should also make sure that the layout meets the approved house style, especially if you have a new member of staff producing the documents for you. The style and format used by the organisation, or by you if there is no house style, should be consistent. Numbers and calculations should be checked individually against the original and totals checked with a calculator.

■ DIY 3.2.2

Write or type the following instruction and order, and then check the text and calculations (use a calculator if you wish). Indicate any corrections, using the approved correction signs.

Please place an order for the foolowing items of stationary.	
2 boxes envalopes at £5.20 a box	£10.40
20 reams of A4 paper, bond at £2.80 each	£54.00
12 boxes of black pens at £3.40 a box	£41.80
1 box of correction fluid (12 bottles)	£8.50
2 rolls of brown paper at £1.20 roll	£2.40
Do not forget to take off the 20% discount we recieve.	
I made the total, after discount, to be £92.88, get the company to deliver in 12 days.	

You should be able to find five textual errors and three numeric errors.

If you have any doubts about the content of the text, check it with the author or the supervisor. Do not assume that what you have been given is always right, as many people make mistakes, especially when things are done in a hurry.

To help you check important or urgent documents it is useful to have the assistance of a reader. This is someone who reads the original document while you check the typewritten one or the other way around. If no-one is available, you may wish to use a ruler on the original or the copy to make sure that you do not jump a line when looking to and from the two documents.

Any corrections made should be unobtrusive and should certainly not lead to any confusion. Do not forget that your documents are part of the organisation's image and are a reflection of you and the standards you accept.

▶ *When should apostrophes be used?*

Apostrophes can easily be misused. The rules state that they should be used to form possessive nouns, that is to show who or what something belongs to, eg:

Carly's pencil
Natalie's lunch box
Leila's coat

If the noun ends in 's' the apostrophe is placed after the 's' and another 's' is added, eg:

Kris's bike

If the noun is a plural, the apostrophe would still be after the 's', eg:

the doctors' surgery

This would mean more than one doctor; if it were the doctor's surgery, then it would mean there was only one doctor. Some nouns are changed slightly when becoming plural instead of adding 's'. Words such as **child** and **woman** become **children** and **women**, and in these cases the apostrophe would appear before the 's' is added, eg:

the children's socks
the women's handbags

An apostrophe is also used when a letter or letters are missed from a word. Words such as don't, you're, aren't, can't, haven't, we've and I've.

■ DIY 3.2.3

Copy out the following sentences and put the apostrophes in the correct place.

1 The childs dress lay on the bed surrounded by paper.
2 The childrens party starts at 3.00 pm but Ive yet to confirm it.

3 Weve got to hurry or well be late.
4 No doubt youve got a good explanation or well report you.
5 Peters pocket was full of berries, nuts and crisps.
6 Its too late to worry, well have to wait until tomorrow.

You should have placed 10 apostrophes in these sentences.

Apart from a dictionary, another useful reference book is a good Thesaurus. This gives alternative words with the same meaning, and can help widen your written and verbal vocabulary. A Glossary gives a specialised list of words and their meanings and is often included at the end of a technical book, for example those used in your particular business. You will also find a general office reference book useful such as *Chambers Office Oracle* or *The Secretary's Handbook*, or *The Secretary's Desk Book* and *Whitaker's Almanack.*

■ DIY 3.2.4

Visit your local library and make a list of all the reference books that would be useful to you when working in a general office to assist with grammar, punctuation, spelling, or give general advice in layout and document production. List down the title, author(s), publishers, date of publication, ISBN number (the international standard book number) cost (if known) and how it would be useful to you.

Completing Element 3.2

To complete this element on checking and marking errors on documents, you will need to put all your DIY tasks in your folder and carry out a final assessment. This assessment must cover a minimum of 10 different documents on several different occasions (three occasions would be enough). The documents could be letters, memos, tables, invoices, orders, reports, etc, and should include typed documents, computer printouts and some handwritten materials.

You will obviously be checking the documents you produce throughout your period of training and these could be used as evidence, as long as you remember to use the approved correction signs and place the corrected document in your folder. If you use documents from work experience make sure that you ask permission first and do not use any material that is confidential or private.

Claiming credit

Once you have completed your final assessment, you will need to write in your record book or folder *how, when, where* and *what* you have done to prove that you are competent. If you hold a typewriting certificate you may be able to claim credit for this, so discuss this with your tutor.

The following is an example of how one trainee completed this claim.

3.2.a During the last 10 weeks in my WP lessons I have read 10 different documents and marked the errors using the approved correction signs (see my folder).

3.2.b I checked all the numbers against the original and I checked calculations with a calculator.

3.2.c I made sure the documents were clearly marked by writing the signs in the margin and in the text.

3.2.d I made sure the layout followed the house style, which was semi-blocked.

3.2.e When I was unsure of the content I checked with the supervisor, or looked up the word in the dictionary. If necessary an amendment was made.

■ Element 3.3

UPDATE RECORDS IN A COMPUTERISED DATABASE

There are two main parts to any computer system, the hardware and the software.

▶ *What is hardware?*

The hardware is the actual computer machinery: the screen (or VDU – visual display unit); keyboard; processor (or CPU – central processing unit); disk drives and the printer.

The CPU is the part of the machine which reads the information (data) and the disks in the disk drives store the information. The CPU will contain a hard disk (also called a fixed disk) which cannot be removed from the machine. It will also have one or two slots in the casing to insert floppy disks to store the information externally. The drives that contain the disks are usually called C for the hard drive, and A and B for the floppy disk drives. Other drives may be created but this is not

Fig 3.10 Computer hardware, with two boxes containing disks for software

important for this unit. You would only need to know about making extra drives if you intended becoming a computer technician or programmer.

▶ *What is software?*

Software is the program that make the hardware work. The programs are supplied on floppy disks, which are usually 3.5" or 5.25" in diameter and are protected by a cover of either hard or soft plastic. The disk itself is visible and looks like a dark brown, smooth, circular piece of plastic – it should not be touched or it will be damaged. Programs are written in languages that the CPUs can understand. The most common of these computer languages are BASIC (Beginner's All-purpose Symbolic Instruction Code) and COBOL (COmmon Business Orientated Language). You will not need to understand these languages unless you intend to become a computer programmer. Most of the people who use computers do not understand how they work, only how to operate the programs which they use.

■ DIY 3.3.1

Look at the machinery you use at work or college. Can you identify all the hardware – the VDU, CPU, keyboard, drives and printer?

Make a list of all the software available to you. You may not be able to use all of it yet, but later you can return to this list and tick off the ones you have learnt to use.

Most of the programs used in a business or college are loaded from the floppy disks to the hard drive. This is called installing a program. The program can then easily be used on a daily basis without having to reload it every time. Each time a program is loaded on to the hard drive, it uses up space and a hard drive will have a limited amount of space. Therefore it can only hold so many programs at one time. The number of programs held depends on the size of the program and the size of the hard drive.

▶ *Looking after the equipment*

On page 75 we discussed how to clean the parts of the computer. You should also check that the screen is placed at a comfortable distance from the keyboard, to make sure you do not suffer from eyestrain. Also make sure you alter the brightness of the screen to suit you, using the brightness control and the contrast control. The screen should be facing away from windows, or direct artificial light, to reduce the glare. If this is not possible, an anti-glare screen may be attached. There should be sufficient space around your keyboard to place your work and to use a mouse or joystick.

■ DIY 3.3.2

Make a health and safety checklist for equipment, including your computer (all parts), and your chair and desk. Type the list and check your own equipment and that of a friend. Does it meet all the requirements? An example is shown in Fig 3.11.

Equipment	Check	Yes	No	Suggested Alteration
desk	correct height			
	adjustable			
	enough space			
	correct light			

Fig 3.11 Health and safety checklist

▶ *How should you look after disks?*

Floppy disks are fragile. They can easily be damaged and damage may result in losing all the information you have stored on them. The information is stored on the disks in tracks, which are similar to the grooves on a record, each track having a circle which can hold a certain amount of information. Disks may be single-sided or double-sided. Double-sided disks can store information on both sides, therefore storing more information than single-sided disks. Disks can also be single or double density, the density of the disk referring to the amount of information that can be stored. If the disk is double density, twice as much information can be stored on it as on a single density disk. The speed at which the CPU runs will depend on which type of disk you can use. It is similar to a video recorder where if you halve the speed at which the tape runs through the machine, you can store twice as much.

The 5.25" disk covers are flexible plastic, but should never be bent. As mentioned earlier, all disks are protected by a plastic cover. The top of the disk is smooth and has no edges, while underneath three edges have been folded over and electronically 'stapled' in place. The

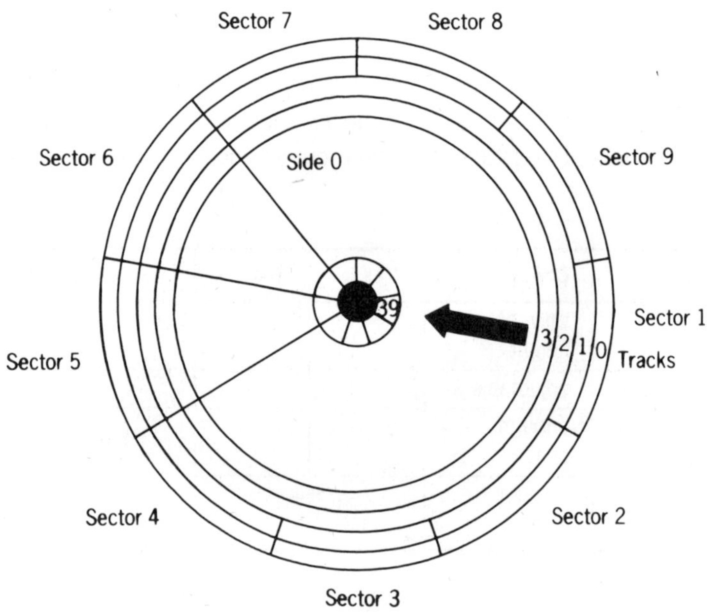

Fig 3.12 Disk track diagram

exposed parts of the disk should be in the middle and an oval slot on one side. This oval slot is on the side which should be pushed first into the disk slot in the casing of the CPU.

The 3.5" disk is protected by a hard plastic cover which has an arrow printed on the front to indicate which way it should be inserted into the CPU disk drive. It also has a metal protection cover over the exposed part of the disk – slide it back carefully to see the disk.

Both these disks may also be called diskettes. Before any disk can be used for storing information it will need to be formatted (sometimes called initialising). Formatting a disk prepares it to accept information from the system you are running on your computer. It is usually done by using the 'format' command, but you will need to check with your supervisor or tutor before you carry out a format on equipment with which you are unfamiliar. If you format an existing disk all the information already stored on it will be lost, as formatting cleans the disk completely.

▶ *Protecting the information on your disk*

On the 5.25" disk you will see a small rectangular cut in the left-hand

Fig 3.13 A 3.5" disk

side. This is the write protection notch. If you do not want to put any further information on the disk or you want to make sure you do not delete any of the information you have on the disk, you can stick a label over the notch. This will then stop you from storing or deleting any further information, as the CPU will not accept changes to that disk.

On the 3.5" disk at the bottom right-hand corner at the back of the disk you will see a small plastic square that will slide up and down. In the up position, the disk would be write protected. (It is rather like breaking off the plastic square from the video tape cassette to stop anyone from recording over it.)

Another way of protecting information stored on a disk is by saving the file with a password or keyword. Before the CPU will allow you to look at the information stored or to delete the file it will be necessary to type in the password. If you use passwords, make sure you remember them. If you write them down, make sure it is somewhere that is not easily found by everyone else in the office. Check before starting your own system that your organisation does not have regulations regarding the use of passwords.

▶ *Labelling your disks*

To protect the exposed areas of the 5.25" disk you should place it in a paper cover and store all disks in a disk box. This may be a small box which can store 5–10 disks, or a desktop box which can store many more. Each of the disks should be labelled, and it is useful to put the label in the corner which you hold when placing the disk into the CPU. When placed in the disk box the labels should be in the top left-hand corner.

Always write on the label *before* you stick it on to the disk. If you need to change the writing on the label of a 5.25" disk at a future date, you can use a fibre tipped pen, but do not use biro or pencil as the pressure of writing on the label may damage the disk.

▶ *Using your disks in the CPU*

To insert a 5.25" disk into the CPU, hold the label and insert the disk into the slot before pushing the lever down into position. To insert a

3.5" disk into the CPU, hold the disk in the right-hand corner and push it into the slot until it clicks down into place.

▶ *Protecting your disks from damage*

The disk box should be kept in a dry place which does not become too hot or cold and should not be exposed to intensive light. The disks should also be kept away from the top of the CPU, from telephones, electrical equipment, steel or any magnetic surface as these may corrupt your disk (even a steel knife and fork could corrupt a disk). A corrupted disk may mean that you will be unable to get your data back, but you should check with a computer technician as they will have access to special programs that can retrieve data or repair damaged disks. Data could also be lost through accidentally deleting a file, overloading or handling the disk.

■ DIY 3.3.3

Complete the following sentences as fully as possible to show that you understand computer equipment and terms.

1 The CPU is ....
2 Formatting is ....
3 A corrupted disk is one that ....
4 Disks should be protected by ....
5 Disk drives are usually called drive .... for the hard disk, and .... for the floppy disk drive. A second floppy disk drive would be called ....

Back-up copies. To reduce the chance of losing your data through a corrupted disk, it is usual to make 'back-up' copies. This means that you keep a copy of the data on a second disk. In some businesses there is a set procedure for making back-up copies, so check with your supervisor at work or ask your tutor how frequently you should make back-ups. Even hard disks may get corrupted so do not rely on keeping all your data on hard disk only. For this reason some businesses change their hard disks and have back-up copies of them, especially if they are dealing with a vast number of pieces of information every day.

■ DIY 3.3.4

Design a leaflet for two juniors, who will be working with you on work experience for three weeks, informing them of how to look after disks. Include handling, storage and protection, labelling, write protecting and backing-up. If possible type your leaflet, but otherwise make sure that it is suitable for use in the office, ie it should be formally presented. If you wish, use labelled diagrams to help explain the points made, or cut out pictures from a supplies catalogue to illustrate your leaflet.

▶ *Saving your data*

It is important to save your data regularly. If you are working all day on the same document, you may save it every half an hour or so. This is just to make sure that you do not lose all the work, for example through someone accidentally switching off your computer or through an electrical power cut. Some programs remind you to save your work by flashing a message at you while you are working, and also by slowing the system down, so you save quickly to enable you to get on! Some programs will create a back-up for you and save automatically every 20 minutes or so.

To save a file it is necessary to give it a filename, which is used to recall the file when you wish to edit or change the information. The names you choose for files may depend on the organisation's policy or they may be entirely up to you. However, if the choice is yours try to have a system that is logical and easy to remember.

The filename will usually indicate the content of the file, and should contain no more than eight characters (preferably only letters as in some programs numbers and other characters have special meanings to the computer). Some databases are also particular about whether small letters or capital letters are typed. Therefore, if you decide to call your file JUMPERS, and when you want to call the file back you enter the file name as jumpers, you may not be able to find it. This is called 'case specific', because the computer is looking for a particular 'case', ie lower case instead of upper case letters.

The second part of the filename is called an extension. Your computer will automatically issue an extension to your file. Those that may appear in your computer file listings will probably include:

.COM command files that inform the computer how to run the program

.EXE executable files which are similar to command files and contain instructions to the CPU

.BAT batch files that contain lists of commands

.SYS system files that contain information about your hardware

.DOC document files that contain the information you have put in

.DBF database files

The last two extensions will be the ones with which you have most contact. You do not need to worry about remembering the extension filenames, but you should keep a record of the filenames you allocate to your data.

▶ *What type of programs are you likely to use?*

The type of programs you are likely to use in an office will be accounts packages, word processing, diary planners and databases. In a specialised department they may also use spreadsheets and statistical packages for processing figures, financial packages for forecasting and running a business; or computer aided design (CAD) packages. These CAD packages assist in drawing and estimating and are commonly used in the drawing offices of engineers and designers. You will probably already have used a word processing package and be familiar with some of the functions.

▶ *Database programs*

A database package is similar to a filing system, in that it stores information and allows you to retrieve it at a later date. You can add a new file or delete an old one. If you have already covered Unit 1, you will have filed items in an alphabetical order. The computer does not need you to sort the information, as it can do this for itself. This means that you can put the information into the computer in any order, and when you add a file it does not have to be at a particular place. Many different organisations use databases to store all sorts of information. They could be used to store customer names and addresses, staff or patients' information, stock records, properties for sale, membership records, etc.

The type of information required for each database will vary and you will need to look carefully at the information to be stored before you create a database. Each piece of information needs to have a line of its own, and this line is called a **field**. For example, if you were creating a database of your relations' birthdays, you would probably want a field for name, one for the day, one for the month, another for the year – four fields altogether. If you wanted to include the address, you might wish to have further fields for street, town, county and postcode.

The computer is able to sort out for you the files stored with a common field. For instance, if you wished to have a list of all the relations who had birthdays in May, you would be able to **list** these by requesting the computer to **sort** out all the files that have May in the field called month.

The fields will be listed on the screen in the shape of a **form**. The information for the relations' or friends' birthdays would therefore look like that shown in Fig 3.14.

Name
Day
Month
Year
Street
Town
County
Postcode

Fig 3.14 Database for information on birthdays

The space you need for each field will depend on the information you intend putting in it. For the name field, you will have to make sure that it is long enough to type in the longest name. The date will only need a maximum of two spaces as the numbers will be between 1–31. The month field will require a maximum of 11 spaces, as September is the longest month (or only two spaces if the month is typed numerically, ie October would be 10). The year would only require four spaces. Usually the database program will indicate by dots, dashes or a block how much space has been reserved in a field.

You will also need to tell the computer the type of information which you will be putting into the field, ie alphabetic letters, numbers or a combination of both. In our example on page 106, the first field is the name, which would be alpha; the second field is the date, which would be numeric. The 'street' field would be alphanumeric, as it probably has the number of the house and the name of the street.

■ DIY 3.3.5

Design a database which will contain fields to hold information on your own family or friends. Select your fields (which may include first name, middle name, age, height, weight, date of birth, etc) and then work out how much space you need in each field. Design the required form on a piece of paper by writing the field names and indicating the space allocated to each field. State which would be alpha, numeric or alphanumeric.

You may find that, once you start using your database, the space allocated to a field is not enough. Most programs allow you to change the space, even after you have started saving information.

►*How do you access a database program?*

The database may be on your computer only or it may be connected (networked) to another computer terminal or several hundred terminals (machines). Networked systems are used in large companies and allow many users to access the same information. The networked system would share the same CPU. All the information would be saved centrally on the CPU, although it may be possible to save your particular information on your own floppy disk.

Access to your database will depend on which program you are using and how the computer has been set up. Some computers will have been set up with a menu (a list of items from which you can choose a program), which appears when you switch on. Others will just have a prompt, such as >C: which is waiting for you to enter a command. Find out from your supervisor or tutor how to access the database program installed on your machine and make sure you write it down, so you do not forget.

Your files in the database program must have different names. If you save your family information as FAMILY.DBF you would not use this name for another file. A file with information on the football clubs might be called FOOTBALL.DBF (remember the filename cannot be more than eight characters). DBF is the extension automatically allocated by the computer, and indicates that the file is a DataBase File.

If you were looking at information in the FOOTBALL file and you wished to look at the FAMILY file, you would have to close the FOOTBALL file and open the FAMILY file, as in many database progams you cannot jump from one to the other and have both open at the same time. To open and close files, select the correct option using the cursor keys and then press the Return (Enter) key.

When you enter information (text or numbers) into the database it is important to be accurate, or you may have problems when selecting or looking for particular files. If you wanted to look at all the family records of people that lived in London and you had typed Londen in some of the records, the computer would not be able to find them. Therefore, you should always proof-read on screen after entering text and before going to the next record or saving the file. If you have made an error, it is easy to correct it by using the cursor keys. Go back to the field where the error is, delete it and type in the correction.

■ DIY 3.3.6

Complete the following sentences, writing as much as you can to prove you have understood the terms used.

1 A field is .....
2 A form is .....
3 A file is .....
4 A network is .....
5 A terminal is .....
6 Fields may be alphabetic,... or ...
7 A database filename may have a maximum of – characters and the extension allocated would be ...

▶ *Searching, sorting and retrieving information*

You may wish to search through the records to find a particular form. If so, you can use the 'page down' key or 'next record' option on the database menus. This will allow you to look at each file. If you want to look at a particular record, you can get the computer to 'sort' out the records for you. You will need to tell the database what to look for. To do this you will choose a particular field, such as month, in the FAMILY file. You could ask the computer to look for all the forms that have 'May' in the month field.

Once set up, the computer database program will search for all the records that have May typed in the month field and it will show you on screen how many forms it has found. You can then look through these records on screen or get a printout of them on your printer. If you wanted, you could choose two fields for the computer to sort at the same time, such as all the records that have May in the month field and also have London in the address field. The computer will again show you how many records it has found for you to look through. Once you have found (retrieved) the forms you need, you can write the details down from the screen or get a printout.

▶ *What organisations may use databases?*

Being able to sort forms is one of the main advantages of a database record system over a paper-based system. An estate agent, for instance, could record all the details of the properties for sale. When a customer is looking for a house priced at £80,000 with four bedrooms in Erith, the office clerk could easily find the correct forms. They would state the four special fields (type of property, price, bedrooms, location) and the details. A printout could then be made of all the houses available for the customer.

A club could use the computer to find out which members need to renew their subscriptions each month. Businesses might use a database program to select the customers located in the Luton area, to enable their representatives to call and inform them of a special offer.

Travel agents use databases which are linked nationally to each other and to the main providers of flights and holidays. They can find a holiday in a certain country or for a certain price or date in a few seconds, and inform the customer of the options.

Colleges keep details of their students on a database and are able, for example, to print out all those attending on Tuesday evening for Law.

The uses of databases are many, eg the financial world uses databases to make sure it has the most up-to-date information about stocks and shares. The Stock Exchange computer system is called SEAQ, (Stock Exchange Automated Quotations system). Each marketmaker (dealer in stocks and shares) has a terminal connected to the central computer and business is carried out via the computer. The main computer is continually updated by agencies such as Reuters, Topic and Telerate, who have the latest information on the market movements.

These are just some examples of databases. No doubt you can think of several more uses for databases.

■ DIY 3.3.7

Design a database that could be used by a local Cub or Brownie troop. Include all the fields you think would be useful, stating whether they would be alphabetic, numeric or alphanumeric. Also decide how much space should be allocated to each field.

▶ *How do you add new records to the database?*

To fill out a new form, or to add a record, you should open the file in the normal way for sorting or looking. You will find that your database menu will have an option called 'append', 'add record' or something similar. Select this option and a blank form will appear on the screen. Complete the fields with the necessary information and save the file again. Your new record will then be added to the file. You will need to look at your own database program to see the exact procedure for adding forms, but most databases are very similar.

► *How do you delete a record?*

To delete a record you can either go to the form you wish to delete and delete the page/record, or you may be able to specify a particular field. For example, delete all the records that have London in the town field. The computer will mark the records ready for deletion and when you save and exit the program these records will not be saved. The computer may give you an opportunity to change your mind when you are exiting, and a message may come on screen such as 'Delete all records marked?'.

In reply to this you can answer Y/N (Yes or No). If you reply Y the file will be saved without the marked records, thus deleting them; if you reply N then you can continue to work in the file and the records will not be deleted.

► *Should you back-up database files?*

Most certainly all your records created on the computer should be backed-up, for the reasons discussed earlier. The database will have an option to allow you to do this. Make sure that you back-up regularly, or every time you finish entering new text or deleting files. Some organisations delete all the records from the hard disk at the end of each year and keep a copy of all the records on floppy disk (a College, for example, may do this so that all the new students for the year can be entered on to the system). It is important to remove old files from the computer system and keep as much space free as possible for your new files.

► *Planning and organising your work*

You should make sure that you have all the necessary information before starting to update your database. The information may be supplied to you in different ways. It could be that the company has a form which is completed by hand and the information is taken from the form and typed into the correct database file, form and field.

On the other hand, you may be taking information verbally from customers or clients and entering this directly on to the database while you are speaking on the telephone. If this is the case, you must make doubly sure that the information you have entered is correct before your customer rings off, so always read back to them the information you have entered.

The database is only as good as the users make it. If the information is out of date and inaccurate, it will be of little use to anyone. It is very important to update your database regularly with information as it is received, such as new telephone numbers, changes of address, new requirements from customers, etc.

The information stored may be confidential, in which case access should be restricted to those people that are authorised to use it. Access can be restricted by using passwords without which users cannot enter the program. Each department may be allocated a password or each separate user may have a password. Some systems will also allow users to look at the information but not to change it or delete it.

This system may be used for students' records, where the tutor enters all the information regarding assessments and students are allocated a password which allows them to access their record and look at the results or get a printout of them. Only the tutor can amend the record, and access by other students is restricted as they will not know the password.

Floppy disks can be copied or stolen, so make sure they are kept in the disk box and then locked in a cupboard or drawer. There should be restricted access to the disks. A booking out system should be introduced when confidential disks are taken away from the office.

▶ *Legal requirements for databases*

If you set up a database which has personal information on individuals, then it must be registered with the Data Protection Registrar. The records should not be kept longer than is necessary and proper security procedures should be introduced to make sure only authorised staff have access to the information stored. The information should also be kept up to date and accurate, and never be passed to anyone who may use it for other purposes, eg a list of doctor's patients should not be passed to a mail order firm to allow them to send sales materials out. Further information regarding registration can be obtained from the Post Office or direct from the Data Protection Registrar.

Completing Element 3.3

To complete this element on updating records in a computerised database you will need to put all DIY tasks in your folder and carry out a final assessment. This assessment must include the inputting of at least 30 records on three separate occasions. Do not forget to proof-read your work carefully and make any necessary corrections before saving it. If possible print out the records saved and place them in your folder for the verifier to see.

If you carry this out at work you may be unable to produce the actual records because of the confidentiality of the information. In this case you should write a report on the type of computer used and the name of the database you are familiar with. Give details of the size of the forms, how many fields, and the type of information you entered (alphabetical, numerical, alphanumeric). Include in your report how you access the program, sort, edit and save. Do not forget to cover the rules for back-up disks and security.

Ask your supervisor at work to sign your report as being correct and confirming that you carried out the work. If possible your tutor should visit you at work to observe you as you are carrying out the tasks.

Claiming credit

Once you have completed your final assessment, you will need to write in your record book or folder *how, when, where* and *what* you have done to prove that you are competent. If you hold a computing certificate, you may be able to claim credit for this, so discuss this with your tutor.

The following is an example of how one trainee completed this claim.

3.3.a While working at Coopers & Co (March–April 199–) I accessed the correct field by using the cursor keys to move around the record.

3.3.b After entering the data, I checked it was correct against the original and also checked it was in the correct field.

3.3.c The back-up disks were kept secure at all times in the disk box, and access was restricted to those allowed to use the database and disks.

3.3.d When faults occurred with the printer, or I could not select the field required, I informed my supervisor.

3.3.e I followed the correct method for looking after the equipment and made sure there were no trailing leads. All liquids were kept away from the machine and dust covers used at the end of the day, and the machine unplugged.

UNIT 4
Processing petty cash and invoices

Element 4.1
PROCESS PETTY CASH TRANSACTIONS

▶ *What is petty cash?*

The word 'petty' means 'small' or 'minor', and petty cash means small amounts of cash. In an office small amounts of cash are quite often needed to pay for items such as travel, cleaning materials, string, registered post and stamps, tea/coffee, light bulbs, etc. The amount of cash kept in the office depends on how much is spent in an average week.

The imprest. The person responsible for the book-keeping, usually the chief accountant or chief cashier, will discuss with your supervisor how much cash is used on a regular basis for small items. This amount is called the **imprest** and it is replaced on a regular basis, either weekly or monthly, depending on how quickly the amount is used.

For example, in a small office the maximum amount used on petty cash weekly might be £20. The chief cashier would give £20 to your supervisor at the beginning of the first week. During the week £15 has been actually spent on small items, leaving £5 in the petty cash at the end of the week. The supervisor would go to the cashier and request that £15 be given to the department to replace the money spent and again make the imprest £20. This is called 'restoring the imprest'.

The Cash Book. When the cashier pays an amount to the petty cash officer, an entry will be made in the Cash Book. It will contain the date, the amount and the name of the person to whom the money was paid. A reference number is given to the petty cash officer, which will usually be the page number of the Cash Book on which the entry was made, eg CB3, Cash Book page 3. This reference is used by the petty cash officer when paying out sums against vouchers. The reference number will usually be written in the Folio Number space on the petty cash voucher (*see* Fig 4.1).

▶ *When are payments made from petty cash?*

It depends on the office whether payments are made on request or at a particular time each week. In a small office it is likely that staff will be repaid immediately for sums paid out. However, nothing should be paid unless the member of staff has an authorised petty cash voucher.

■ DIY 4.1.1

Make a list of items that you think may be suitable for petty cash payments. They should be small items that are used in an office or items of which you run out and need to buy a temporary stock while waiting for a large order to be delivered.

▶ *What is a petty cash voucher?*

A petty cash voucher should have detailed on it, the date, the amount requested and a description of the expenditure. It should be signed by the person wanting the repayment and authorised by the supervisor. The voucher should also have any receipts attached to it as proof of the payment made. Unless a request for payment is made with a petty cash voucher, no payment should be made.

If the voucher has been completed correctly, the petty cash officer should enter the folio number and the voucher number (this will be the next number to be allocated) on the petty cash voucher and pay out the amount of cash requested. The numbering system for voucher numbers may start at the beginning of the year, eg 94/1 (year/voucher number), or at the beginning of each month, eg 94/2/1 (year, month, voucher number). The organisation may already have an approved system in use. Otherwise you should discuss with your supervisor which system you wish to use. You will also need to complete the petty cash analysis sheet (this will be discussed later).

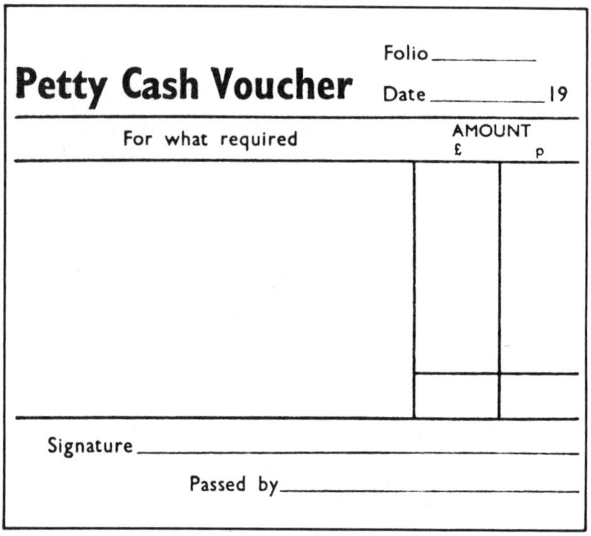

Folio ______

Petty Cash Voucher Date ______ 19

For what required	AMOUNT £	p

Signature ______

Passed by ______

Fig 4.1 A petty cash voucher

■ DIY 4.1.2

Photocopy the blank voucher above, or ask your tutor for a supply of blank vouchers. You will need six for this task. Make out vouchers for the following expenditure:

1. Flowers for reception office, bought on 6 Feb., costing £5.40
2. Tea and coffee for visitors, bought on 7 Feb., costing £3.50
3. Window cleaning carried out on 7 Feb., at a charge of £5.00 plus 88p VAT, totalling £5.88 (show the VAT separately on the voucher)
4. Stamps bought at the Post Office on 8 Feb., totalling £4.00
5. Bus fare paid when delivering an urgent parcel to Head Office on 9 Feb., £1.20
6. The post room ran out of string on 9 Feb. so you bought some which cost £1.20 plus VAT of 21p = £1.41

Sign the vouchers yourself and get your tutor to check and authorise them. Keep the vouchers safe as you will need them later for another task. (The reasons for including VAT (value added tax) in two of your vouchers will be explained then.)

▶ *What if a voucher is not produced?*

Anyone asking you to supply money from the petty cash without an authorised voucher should be referred to your supervisor. It may be that their claim can be approved, such as an office junior who has been asked to get some stamps but does not have the necessary cash. Such an irregularity may be quite usual but the decision to pay the cash must be made by your supervisor and not by you. Some members of staff may ask for a 'loan' (perhaps for their lunch) and these requests should be turned down with a polite but firm 'No'. All the money issued needs to be accounted for. If the accountant or auditors were to choose to check your cash tin, you could be in severe trouble if any cash were 'on loan' to a friend. If you find any money missing, this should be reported immediately to your supervisor and the chief cashier. Any irregularities, or anything that is not routine, should be reported promptly to someone in authority.

▶ *What security measures should you take?*

Each payment from the petty cash must be supported by a petty cash voucher and this will ensure that only approved amounts are paid. In addition, regular checks should be made to ensure the correct amount of cash remains in the tin. It is normal to have a lockable petty cash tin which has two sections, the bottom section keeping all the banknotes and the top section being divided into partitions for the different coins, similar to a cash till in a shop. At the end of every week, or daily if several amounts have been paid out, the money should be counted and checked against your vouchers. The locked tin should be kept in a drawer or cupboard that is also kept locked and only authorised persons should have access to the tin. The keys should be kept in a secure place and this should not be known except by authorised persons. It is also advisable to change the place on a regular basis.

When paying out money, count the sum required from the petty cash tin on to your desk. Then close the tin and count the money out in front of the person requesting it. This helps to reduce mistakes and ensures that the person receiving the money does not claim you gave them the wrong amount. If you are giving change to someone who has given you a banknote, keep the note given to you on the desk until the change has been given and accepted. This is in case someone states that they gave you a higher value note than you thought. Make sure that you enter all payments, in and out, immediately on the analysis sheet (*see* below).

■ DIY 4.1.3

Below you will find sentences that are incomplete. The sentences are relevant to the work you have already covered and the information above. Copy out the sentences, filling in the gaps with the words provided:

authority *restricted* *locked* *petty cash voucher* *cash book*

1 Petty cash should only be paid on the production of a _ _ _ _ _ _ _ _ _ _ _ _ _ _ _ _ _.
2 The petty cash should be kept in a _ _ _ _ _ _ tin.
3 Access to the petty cash should be _ _ _ _ _ _ _ _ _ _.
4 Requests for cash not supported by a voucher should be referred to an appropriate _ _ _ _ _ _ _ _ _.
5 The folio number is the page number from the _ _ _ _ _ _ _ _.

If you have difficulty in completing these, read the above paragraphs again.

▶ *What is an analysis sheet?*

This is a summary of all the petty cash payments made, both in and out. It enables you to check whether the amount in the tin is correct and it is also the document that the chief accountant and auditors (those that examine the company's accounting procedures and documents) will want to check. It is vital that you write clearly and are 100 per cent correct, as the analysis sheet is an important document and needs to be read by several people. Look at the example in Figure 4.2. You can see that the imprest agreed is £20 and this has been entered on 2 January. The folio reference is CB1, which means that the Cash Book entry has been made on page 1. The amount of £20 has been entered on the left-hand side of the analysis sheet (the debit side).

The first voucher to be agreed is voucher number 1 of month 1 (1/1), and it totals £5.50 for magazines which have been bought for the reception area. The amount has been written in the Amount column on the right-hand side of the analysis sheet and also in the Reception column. The second voucher is for milk that has been purchased for

Debit			PETTY CASH ANALYSIS SHEET								Credit
Date	Folio	Amount £ p	Details	V No	Amount £ p	Travel	Stationery	Post	Refresh-ments	Reception	VAT £ p
Jan 2	CB1	20.00	Received cash imprest								
" 3			Magazines for reception	1/1	5.50					5.50	
" 3			Milk	1/2	2.50				2.50		
" 4			Cleaning	1/3	11.75					10.00	1.75
" 5			Total for week		19.75				2.50	15.50	1.75
" 5			Balance cartied down (c/d)		0.25						
		20.00			20.00						
		0.25	Balance brought down (b/d)								
" 8	CB2	19.75	Cash received								

Fig 4.2 Petty cash analysis sheet

the office. This totals £2.50 and the amount has been written in the Amount column and the Refreshments column.

The third voucher is a little different as it has VAT (value added tax) included. VAT is currently set at 17.5% but this amount is reviewed regularly by the Government and may go up or down. The VAT must be shown separately – this is because businesses may be able to get their VAT repaid (if they are registered) and the accountant will wish to know exactly how much VAT you have paid out over the last year. Any amount that includes VAT should be divided by 117.5 and then multipled by 17.5 to find out what the VAT is, eg:

£25 ÷ 117.5 = 0.2127659 x 17.5 = 3.72

To find the original cost of the goods, before VAT was added, divide by 117.5 and multiply by 100, eg:

£25 ÷ 117.5 = 0.2127659 x 100 = 21.28

This means that the original amount of the goods was £21.28 and 17.5% VAT on this is £3.72; add these together and the total amount paid for the goods is £25 (£21.28 + £3.72 = £25).

You will need to practise these formulae until you can remember them!

■ DIY 4.1.4

Using a calculator, work out the VAT contained in the following amounts. Some clues have been given and the answers are below, although they are not in the correct order.

1 £10
2 £12.50
3 £17.50
4 £2.20
5 £1.75

The answers should be: £1.86 £1.48 £2.60 26p 32p

Putting the amounts under the separate headings in the analysis sheet also allows you to double check that your arithmetic is correct. The total paid out for the week (calculated by adding the amount column) should equal the total of all the itemised columns. Each column should be added up and the total written on the same line as the total for the week. If you now add the totals of the itemised columns across the page, the figure should equal the figure in the amount column (do not include the amount column total when adding across). In the example, this would mean adding the Refreshments, Reception and VAT column totals together.

Add up the money left in the petty cash tin. Write this balance in the amount column, below the total paid out for the week. Adding these total and balance figures together should give you the same figure as your original imprest amount (£20 in our example). Carry down the balance figure to the imprest amount column, and then ask the cashier for the cash to give you £20 again to start the next week.

■ DIY 4.1.5

Make a photocopy of the blank analysis sheet (Fig 4.3) on page 122 (or ask your tutor for a blank sheet). You have been asked to run the petty cash while the petty cash officer is on holiday. You are starting a new analysis sheet with an imprest of £25 which has been allocated from the cashier on 1 February. Your folio number is CB6. There is no balance to be brought down from last month. Head the analysis columns with Stationery/Post, Travel, Cleaning, Refreshments, Miscellaneous and VAT. Using the vouchers you prepared in DIY 4.1.2, fill in the folio numbers on your vouchers and allocate voucher numbers which run in order. Enter the details on the analysis sheet. Using a calculator, add up the amount column on the right-hand side and the analysis columns (double check your arithmetic by adding the totals across as well as down). Write in your total amount paid for the week, the balance to carry forward, the total imprest (in both amount columns), and the amount brought forward for the next week (13 February).

How much did you have left in your petty cash tin at the end of the week?

How much do you need from the cashier to restore your imprest?

Completing Element 4.1

To complete this element on petty cash you will need to put all your DIY tasks in your folder and carry out a final assessment. This must cover a minimum of

Debit		PETTY CASH ANALYSIS SHEET								Credit
Date Folio	Amount £ p	Details	V No	Amount £ p						

Fig 4.3

one month's petty cash vouchers and analysis sheet(s). All copies of your vouchers, receipts and records must be presented. You should also be prepared to answer questions about the type of irregularities that may occur while working as a petty cash officer. If you work full-time or part-time and deal with cash, you may be able to get some credit for the security and safety procedures that you carry out. However, you will still need to supply all the documentation for petty cash transactions.

Claiming credit

Once you have completed your final assessment, you will need to write in your record book or folder how, when, where and what you have done to prove that you are competent.

The following is an example of how one trainee completed this claim.

4.1.a During our assignment we learnt that all cash had to be kept in a locked petty cash tin which was kept in a locked drawer. Access to the tin was limited to those people authorised and cash was only issued if a voucher was approved. I also deal with cash in my part-time job at the supermarket and meet all the safety and security procedures required.

4.1.b I recorded all the vouchers on the analysis sheet after putting the folio number and voucher number on the voucher. I checked that each voucher had been signed by a supervisor before being passed for payment. I made sure my writing was neat and readable.

4.1.c When problems arose I referred them to my supervisor/tutor. These problems included a person wanting cash without a voucher, money missing from the tin and someone wanting to borrow cash to pay for their lunch. It was not within my authority to deal with these problems.

■ Element 4.2

PROCESS INCOMING INVOICES FOR PAYMENT

Many organisations have a number of different departments, among which may be the Purchasing Department, Sales Department and Accounts Department. We have already seen some of the work of the Accounts Department in the petty cash section of this chapter.

The work carried out in all these departments should be treated as confidential and when working you should not discuss work outside your department. When working for a business, either as an employee or on work experience, you may find that you know some of the customers or suppliers personally – they may be friends, neighbours or relations. In these circumstances it is even more important to keep all your work confidential, in case a complaint is made to your supervisor or directors about your discussing business out of work.

▶ *What does a Purchasing Department do?*

This department purchases the equipment, raw materials, stationery and supplies required by all the other departments. The staff in the department will be buyers, whose job it is to look for the best deal from all the different suppliers.

An enquiry will be sent out to different suppliers, which will request the price and terms (such as discounts available) for the goods required.

A quotation will be sent back by the supplier, which will give the buyer all the information required to decide whether to buy or not.

An Order will be sent to the supplier requesting the goods once the buyer has decided to buy them.

An acknowledgement may be sent by the supplier to let the buyer know that the order has been received and is getting attention.

An advice note will be sent by the supplier when the goods are ready to be sent. This will give details of when and how the goods will be sent. They may be posted by van or rail, hand delivered or they may have to be collected.

A delivery note will be with the goods when they are received by the buyer. This should contain the same details as the advice note. It is the responsibility of the person receiving the goods to ensure that the goods in the parcels match the details on the delivery note. Any differences must be written on the delivery note and confirmed with the person making the delivery. When the person receiving the goods is happy that the order is correct, he/she will sign the delivery note, keep a copy and return a copy to the person making the delivery, who will return the copy to the supplier. The signed delivery note will be passed to the Purchasing Department, to show that the goods requested have now arrived.

Invoice. When the supplier receives the signed delivery note, the supplier will send an invoice, which is the bill for the goods supplied.

This will give full details of the goods supplied, together with a breakdown of costs, including discounts, delivery and VAT. This document will be sent to the buyer's **Accounts Department**.

▶ *What does the Accounts Department do?*

The Accounts Department is responsible for all the money within the business. The staff employed will usually include a Chief Accountant, who will have Account Clerks to assist in the work. The money in a company is called **capital**. **Working capital** is the money used to buy all the supplies required, pay wages and petty cash. It comes from the customers who buy the goods or services from the company.

Fixed capital is money invested in buildings and equipment, such as machinery and furniture.

The Accounts Department will carry out all the duties connected with looking after the money and try to make sure that the company does not get into debt. If the company is doing well, most of the money coming into it will be from the **Sales Department**.

▶ *What does the Sales Department do?*

The Sales Department will have staff employed who are salespersons (salesmen and saleswomen). They will have skills in being able to sell the goods or services of the company to customers. They will answer **enquiries** from other companies and supply **quotations**, listing the cost of the goods required as well as the terms. Once they receive an **order**, they will send out an **acknowledgement** letting the customer know that the order has been received and is getting attention. When the order is ready to go out, the Sales Department will send an **advice note** to the customer, telling them when and how the goods will be delivered. When the goods are sent, a **delivery note** will be included with them, and this will be checked against the goods by the customer and signed. The signed delivery note will be returned to the Sales Department. When the Sales Department knows that the customer has received the goods and there are no problems, an **invoice** will be sent asking for payment for the goods.

The Accounts Department now brings together the work of the Purchasing Department and the Sales Department. The staff in the

Accounts Department have to make sure that the bills received by the Purchasing Department are paid and will write cheques to cover the amounts. They will also make sure that the customers of the Sales Department pay the bills that have been sent to them. If the Accounts Department fails to do this efficiently, then it may result in cash flow problems for the company, ie more money going out than is coming in.

■ DIY 4.2.1

In your own words complete the sentences below:

1 A Purchasing Department's duties include ....
2 An Accounts Department's duties include ....
3 A Sales Department's duties include ....

Fill the gaps from the information you have read above:

4 A Purchasing Department employs ______ as members of its staff.
5 An Accounts Department employs a _____ ___________ and _________ ______.
6 A Sales Department employs _________ and ___________.

▶ *What records are kept by the departments?*

The Purchasing Department will keep a record of all its suppliers and this will be updated and amended as new and better suppliers are found. It will probably keep a selection of catalogues and may meet with supplier representatives on a regular basis to keep up to date. The buyers will also keep a record of all their enquiries and orders sent. It is important that the buyers inform the Accounts Department of any orders placed, especially if these involve a lot of money, as the Accounts Department will have to pay the bills when they arrive. Usually, therefore, an order form pad is used, each order having a separate number, and a copy of the order is sent to the Accounts Department.

The Accounts Department will keep all the ledgers. These are the books where all the deals (buying and selling) are written down. The department will have a Purchases Ledger and a Sales Ledger, detailing all the orders and sales that the departments have made, with the date, name of customer/supplier, and the amount due/owed. When the payment has been made, the ledger will be updated with the amount and date of payment. Many organisations now use computerised accounts packages to assist with these duties.

The Sales Department will keep records of its customers and the orders they make. They will also be looking for new customers so will probably keep a record of companies or individuals' addresses in the sales area for contact to try to obtain new business. The Sales Department will make sure that the invoice is sent to the customer (detailing the goods, cost, discounts, VAT and time allowed for payment). It is important that the Sales Department keeps the Accounts Department informed as to which customers owe money. This ensures that the Accounts Clerks can follow up any late payments and keep a record of all incoming payments. Usually the invoices are in a pad form with an individual number. A copy of the invoice will be sent to the Accounts Department.

■ DIY 4.2.2

Check your knowledge of the terms used. Copy out the following sentences and fill in the correct word from those supplied:

advice note *enquiry* *invoice* *delivery note* *sign*
acknowledgement *order*

1 A Purchasing Department will send out an _ _ _ _ _ _ _ to find out the cost of goods and terms. If they are happy they will place an _ _ _ _ _ for the goods.

2 When the supplier receives an order they will send an _ _ _ _ _ _- _ _ _ _ _ _ _ _ _ _ to let the customer know the order has been received.

3 When the goods are ready for despatch the supplier will send an _ _ _ _ _ _ _ _ _ _ to the customer to let him/her know the date and type of delivery.

4 When the goods are received, the customer will check the _ _ _ _ _ _ _ _ _ _ _ _ _ against the goods. When the customer is happy, he/she will _ _ _ _ the note, keep a copy and return a copy to the person making the delivery.

5 Once the supplier knows the goods have been received and that the customer is happy, an _ _ _ _ _ _ _ will be sent, detailing the cost of the goods and how much is owed. This is also known as the bill.

More information about these documents and the procedures involved can be found in Unit 5, Stock handling, on pages 134–5.

► *Checking*

One of the most important jobs in the organisation is checking that **invoices** are correct. First the invoice must be checked against the **delivery note**. Whoever received the goods should have checked them against the delivery note and signed to say it was correct, or written on the note what was wrong. If an order is too big to check at the time, or the person receiving the goods is too busy, the delivery note may be signed 'Goods received but not checked'. A copy of the signed delivery note should be available to the Accounts Department to check against the invoice when it arrives. If there are any items on the invoice that were not received, then the supplier needs to be informed. In the same way, if there are any items on the delivery note that have not been included in the invoice, the supplier should be informed.

If you carry out these important duties you will probably have a supervisor who can assist you when you have any queries. If you discover any differences on the invoice or delivery note, you should report these promptly. Your supervisor will probably double check the discrepancies before informing the supplier.

■ DIY 4.2.3

Check the following delivery note (Fig 4.4) against the invoice (Fig 4.5) received in your department. Make a note of any differences and write a memo to your supervisor setting out your findings. Say whether you have approved the invoice for payment or whether the supplier needs to be contacted.

When checking an invoice, in addition to checking it against the delivery note you should also check the calculations. Make sure that you use a calculator for this. If more than one of the same item has been ordered, you will need to check that the total charged is correct. You will also need to check the addition and any VAT charged. VAT is currently charged at 17.5 per cent, but this may change when the Government reviews its budget. Some items do not have VAT charged on them (some are exempt and others zero rated, ie 0 per cent VAT), and you will need to check with your accounts department whether an item has VAT or not. Examples of items that do not have VAT included at the moment are most foods, books, children's clothes and children's shoes.

DELIVERY NOTE

To: D & G Scaffolding
Wimborne
BH2 9JJ

Date: 26 May

Quantity	Description	Price
2 packs	A4 Yellow Executive Pads	–
10 packs	A4 Typing Paper	–
1 pack	Manilla Envelopes 9"x 4"	–
10	Box Files	–
1	Postal Scales & Adaptor	–

Goods received..Signed

Fig 4.4

INVOICE

To: D & G Scaffolding
Wimborne
BH2 9JJ

Invoice No. 1029
Date: 12 June

Quantity	Description	Price
2 packs	A4 Yellow Executive Pads @ £5·65 each	11-30
10 packs	A4 Typing Paper @ £1·89 each	18-90
1 pack	Manilla Envelopes 9"x 4"	10-95
20	Box Files @ £3·25 each	65-00
1	Postal scales	59-95
		166-10
	+VAT @ 17·5%	29-07
	TOTAL DUE	195-17

Payment required within 30 days./Cash received*
E&OE
*Delete as appropriate

Fig 4.5

■ DIY 4.2.4

Check the delivery note on page 131 (Fig 4.6) against the invoice (Fig 4.7), making sure that you use your calculator. List the discrepancies found and draft a letter of apology to the customer.

Completing Element 4.2

To complete this element on processing incoming invoices for payment, you will need to put all DIY tasks in a folder and carry out a final assessment. The assignment must cover a minimum of 10 invoices (routine and non-routine) which must be checked against delivery notes. The work must be carried out on three separate occasions. You will also be expected to answer questions about the use and purpose of invoices.

Claiming credit

Once you have completed your final assessment, you will need to write in your record book or folder how, when, where, and what you have done to prove that you are competent.

The following is an example of how one trainee completed this claim:

4.2.a I checked at least 10 delivery notes against the invoices and made a list of all the differences.

4.2.b I used a calculator to check the calculations on the invoices and any errors were noted in pencil on the invoice.

4.2.c Errors I found between the delivery notes and the invoices, and in the calculations, were written down and reported to the supervisor promptly.

4.2.d If invoices were correct, I passed them for payment; if incorrect, the errors were identified.

4.2.e I made sure that all the records I used were up to date and that my writing was readable.

These duties were carried out in my part-time job at News Around paper shop – see folder for evidence.

DELIVERY NOTE

To D & G Scaffolding — Date July 7th
Wimborne
BH2 9JJ

Quantity	Description	Price
6 rolls	Fax paper 24G-M-T	—
20 disks	3·5 DD 226/19	—
5	"Tru" Highlighters 223/22	—
2	Four hole punch	—
20	Shorthand notebooks	—

Goods received...Signed

Fig 4.6

INVOICE

To D & G Scaffolding — Invoice No. 1925
Wimborne — Date August 10th
BH2 9JJ

Quantity	Description	Price
6 rolls	Fax paper 24G-0-T @£3·29 roll	23-03
20 disks	3·5 HD 226/19 £12-99 box 10	25-98
10	"Tru" Highlighters 222/22 64p each	6-40
2	Four hole punch @£14-99 each	14-99
20	Shorthand Notebooks @£2-99 each pack 10	7-47
		92-86
	+VAT@17·5%	16-25
	TOTAL DUE	109-11

Payment required within 30 days./Cash received*
E&OE
*Delete as appropriate

Fig 4.7

UNIT 5
Stock handling

▪ Element 5.1
ISSUE OFFICE MATERIALS ON REQUEST AND MONITOR STOCK LEVELS

Have you ever heard the terms 'stocktake', 'out of stock' or 'summer/winter stock'? The term 'stock' has the same general meaning, whether in a large industrial organisation or a small office. In the *Pocket Oxford Dictionary* it is described as 'Store of goods, etc, ready for sale, distribution, or use, supply of anything'.

In your college or workplace you will find different kinds of stock. This stock is usually kept together in a special place called a storeroom, stockroom, or 'the stores'. The stock is kept here to protect it and to make sure it is ready to be taken out when required. You must always remember that stock is worth money; it is of value to the organisation and you must treat it with great care.

▶ *What types of stock are there?*

The stock held by any organisation will generally fall into one of five categories:

1 Raw materials

This type of stock is held ready for use in the manufacture of goods. Sufficient stock of raw materials and components must be held for a regular supply to the production department. Can you imagine what would happen if the production department was brought to a halt because there were not enough raw materials in stock to make the goods? Examples of raw materials would be cocoa in a chocolate factory or cotton and other textiles in a clothing manufacturer's factory.

2 Consumables

These are supplies that are necessary for the smooth running of the organisation, but which are used up in the day-to-day running of the business and do not make a profit in themselves. Consumables may be used up quickly so there must always be a reserve in stock. Examples of consumables in an office would be stationery, such as envelopes, rulers and notebooks.

3 Finished goods

These are the goods that have been manufactured by the organisation and are held in stock awaiting orders from customers. The organisation will want to sell this stock as quickly as possible to make a profit, in order to buy more raw materials and make more finished goods. The organisation will always keep in stock popular lines which sell quickly, so that delivery can be made upon the receipt of an order – this is called delivery 'ex-stock'. Examples of finished goods are cars, bicycles, computers, furniture and carpets.

4 Goods purchased for resale

Retail shops and wholesale warehouses purchase a variety of stock which they display and hope to sell at a higher price than they paid the manufacturer, to make a profit. These outlets usually offer a wide range of stock from which customers can choose as and when they require it. Examples of resale stock would be clothing, food and drink, and electrical equipment.

5 Spare parts

These are required so that they are readily available in the event of the breakdown of the factory machinery, vehicles, plant, etc. Examples of spare parts would be engines, gear boxes, and smaller items such as nuts and bolts, and fan belts.

■ DIY 5.1.1

Prepare a table entitled 'Types of stock'. Down the left-hand side of the page list the five types of stock already mentioned. Next to each heading across the page give two of your own examples, together with details of the type of organisation that might use them.

▶ *How might stock be ordered?*

The stock used in your organisation will be purchased from suppliers (retail shops, wholesalers or manufacturers). The organisation will send out an initial **enquiry**, perhaps to three or four suppliers, in order to find out which supplier can offer the best deal. In return the suppliers will send a **quotation** detailing the goods required and the price and terms that they are prepared to offer. The supplier may also take this opportunity to send price lists, catalogues and free samples, or arrange for a sales representative to call.

The purchasing department will decide upon the supplier to use and will send out an **order**. When the supplier receives this order, an **acknowledgement** will be sent back to the organisation's purchasing department to confirm that the supplier has received the order. Once the order is ready to be delivered, the supplier will send an **advice note** by post, containing the delivery details for the goods.

A delivery note, containing the same details as the advice note, will be sent with the goods. It is the responsibility of the person receiving these goods to ensure that the goods correspond with the goods detailed in the delivery note. Any discrepancies must be written down on the delivery note and confirmed by the signatures of the persons delivering and receiving the goods.

An invoice will be produced by the supplier for each delivery of goods sent to the organisation. This will give full details of the goods supplied, together with a breakdown of costs, including any discounts (money off) and VAT. At the end of each month the supplier will send the organisation a **statement** which details the amount payable for all the invoices for that month, less any refunds for goods returned or damaged. The organisation then arranges for a **cheque** to be sent to the supplier in settlement of the account.

This process will be used when an organisation is first looking for a supplier of a particular range of goods. Once contact has been made and a suitable supplier found, it is usual for the organisation to place regular orders with the same supplier. However, in the case of an emergency supply being required at short notice, most suppliers will take an order over the telephone. This should, however, be supported by giving them an order number, and an authorised order form should be sent by post or fax as soon as possible.

In the case of smaller organisations you may find yourself being sent in person to collect goods which are urgently required.

DIY 5.1.2

In order to help you to remember this sequence for ordering stock, copy out on a piece of paper the diagram shown below, and then fill in the lines with the names of the relevant documents.

Buyer	Seller
E ________________	
	Q ________________
O ________________	
	A ________________
	A ________________
	D ________________
	I ________________
	S ________________
C ________________	

▶ *Checking*

It is usual practice to check deliveries against the initial order, to ensure that the correct goods and quantities are being delivered. The delivery note (complete with corrections if there any) will then be compared against the invoice sent to your organisation, to make sure the correct amount has been charged.

If at any stage a mistake is identified, this must be reported to a supervisor immediately. It may be that incorrect goods have been delivered, which will need to be returned, or that your organisation has been charged for goods that it has not received. In both cases it may be your responsibility to find these errors and mark them on the delivery note before signing it. Remember that the delivery company uses the delivery note as a receipt for goods delivered and will, therefore, work out your organisation's final invoice based on these details.

■ DIY 5.1.3

Compare the following order forms (Fig 5.1a) with their delivery notes (Fig 5.1b). Make a list of all the errors you find, writing the correct details next to each error.

Often organisations use stationery packs which contain all the relevant documents for one order. Each document is either made from NCR (no carbon required) paper, or will have carbon paper placed between each sheet. When the order details are typed or written on to the top sheet they are automatically copied on to the other sheets – delivery note, stores requisition, accounts advice, invoice, and so on.

This saves time, as the documents do not have to be prepared separately. Sections of information that are not needed on certain forms can be blanked out (for example, it is usual practice not to have price details on the delivery form).

▶ *Why do organisations hold stock?*

It is essential to have a reserve supply of all the goods and materials required for your organisation to operate efficiently. Delays in the supply of such stock will cause hold-ups in production and possible loss of profits if an order cannot be delivered on time.

Another point to remember is that it is cheaper to order goods in 'bulk' and put the excess into stock so that advantage can be taken of discounts and lower prices. However, care must be taken not to over-order. Remember that stock is worth money to an organisation and a storeroom full of stock that is not used for a long time is tying up money that could be used elsewhere.

▶ *What quantity of stock is usually held?*

This will vary according to the type of organisation, size of organisation, and how much business is carried out. There are also five other very important considerations.

PEMBROOKE MARKETING SERVICES LTD

115–119 Cavendish Square, Bridport, BR4 9PQ

Order Number: 123890 Date: 12.9.– –

Please supply the items listed below:

Quantity	Description	Cat. No.	Unit Price £	Total Price £
12	Pencils	16354		10.69
4	Markers (red)	11987	0.60	2.40
4	Markers (green)	11988	0.60	2.40
4	Markers (yellow)	11989	0.60	2.40
10	Reams A4 Bond (white)	20675	4.15	41.50
2	Reams A4 Bank (yellow)	20667	4.10	8.20
			TOTAL	67.59
	Authorised by A N Other			

PEMBROOKE MARKETING SERVICES LTD

115–119 Cavendish Square, Bridport, BR4 9PQ

Order Number: 123892 Date: 15.10.– –

Please supply the items listed below:

Quantity	Description	Cat. No.	Unit Price £	Total Price £
12	Pencils	19875		10.69
2	Staplers	35627	5.95	11.90
5	Sticky tape	36728	0.98	4.90
24	Correction fluid	09758	1.54	39.96
7	Staple removers	67301	1.37	9.59
			TOTAL	77.04
	Authorised by A N Other			

Fig 5.1a

The Stationery Company Ltd

97 Fontmell Street
Bridport Dorset

Date: 20 September 199–

Order No: 123890 Delivery Note No: 1675

Delivery Address: Pembrooke Marketing Services
115–119 Cavendish Street
Bridport

Quantity	Description of goods	Catalogue number	Total £
12	Pencils	16354	10.69
4	Red markers	11987	2.40
4	Yellow markers	11989	2.40
5	Blue markers	11986	3.00
10	A4 Bank white	10675	31.50
20	A4 Bank yellow	20667	82.00

Please mark errors or damaged goods before signing

....

Do not pay until you have received our official invoice.

The Stationery Company Ltd

97 Fontmell Street
Bridport Dorset

Date: 27 September 199–

Order No: 123892 Delivery Note No: 1897

Delivery Address: Pembrooke Marketing Services
115–119 Cavendish Street
Bridport

Quantity	Description of goods	Catalogue number	Total £
12	Pencils	16354	10.69
5	Staplers	35627	29.75
5	Sticky tape	36728	5.90
24	Staple removers	67301	32.88
7	Correction Fluid	09758	10.78

Please mark errors or damaged goods before signing

....

Do not pay until you have received our official invoice.

Fig 5.1b

1 Money

You are already aware that stock is worth money and that it would be unwise for an organisation to have too much money tied up in stock. It is also wise to remember that some stock may be perishable and have a limited shelf-life. Stock may become dated and therefore unsaleable, or it may age with time and become unusable. Examples are fashionable clothing, fruit and vegetables, and even paper, which may become yellow in time.

2 Time

It may be difficult, or indeed impossible, to obtain stock immediately and valuable orders may be lost to other organisations who are able to deliver the goods on the date required. You will find that, to prevent this situation arising, most organisations will carry a sufficient amount of stock to ensure that when orders are received they can be fulfilled immediately.

3 Space

The storage of stock is expensive. It uses valuable space in areas which must be maintained, heated, protected and secured. Staff are employed to take charge of stock and insurance must be paid to provide cover in the event of damage. The organisation will anticipate the maximum amount of each item of stock that should be kept at one time to prevent profits being spent purely on storage costs.

4 Sales

The organisation will anticipate the actual quantity of stores, spares, raw materials, etc, it will need to keep itself operational. While it is important not to carry too much stock, it is more important to ensure that there is enough stock available to prevent production being halted and money lost.

5 Usage

It is very important to have a regular supply of the stock that is used most often. In an office you might find yourself needing typewriter cartridges, lift-off tapes, paper and envelopes on a regular basis. A clothes manufacturer would need material, sewing cotton and zips/ buttons readily at hand in order to keep production going.

Therefore, it is usual to find that regular orders are placed for high-usage items so that they do not run out.

■ DIY 5.1.4

Below you will find sentences that are incomplete. The sentences are relevant to the work already covered. Copy out these sentences and fill in the missing word(s) which you can select from the following:

1 *time sales space money*
2 *purchases reserve supply production*
3 *consumables purchased paper raw materials spare parts finished goods components*

1 The quantity of stock an organisation would hold at any one time would depend upon:
a Cost of _ _ _ _ _ which includes insurance, heating, etc.
b The amount of _ _ _ _ _ so they do not run out of goods.
c _ _ _ _ taken for the delivery of goods from supplier.
d The _ _ _ _ _ available for the purchase of stores.

2 a Stock is held in the stores to provide a _ _ _ _ _ _ _ _ _ _ _ _ _ of materials needed for the efficient running of an organisation.
b Stock is the result of _ _ _ _ _ _ _ _ _ _ and _ _ _ _ _ _ _ _ _ _ _.

3 There are five types of stock used by organisations.

a _ _ _ _ _ _ _ _ _ _ _ _ _ and _ _ _ _ _ _ _ _ _ _ _ are examples of stock waiting to be turned into manufactured goods.
b _ _ _ _ _ _ _ _ _ _ _ _ _ _ are those which have been manufactured by the organisation for sale.
c _ _ _ _ _ _ _ _ _ _ _ _ for example _ _ _ _ _ are used in the running of the business, but are not profitable.
d _ _ _ _ _ _ _ _ _ _ would be held by an organisation in case of breakdown.
e And lastly, stock may be goods _ _ _ _ _ _ _ _ _ _ for resale at a higher price in order to make profit.

▶ *Why is it necessary to keep control of stock?*

Small organisations may use a 'visual' system of stock control – in other words, stock is ordered when a need is seen. Larger organisations, especially those involved in manufacturing, use a 'bin' system where all components are given a bin number which identifies the component's position in the storeroom. However, most organisations will use 'stock cards' as a system of keeping an up-to-date record of the stock in hand.

A stock card (*see* Fig 5.2) will show details of each item used by the organisation (**1**). Each time stock is delivered by a supplier this will be *added on* to the record (**2**), and each time stock is issued to a department in response to a **stock requisition form**, this is *deducted* from the record (**3**), thus showing exactly how much is in stock at any one time (**4**).

We have already discussed how important it is for an organisation not to have too much stock or too little stock. To prevent either of these situations arising a stock record card is used to indicate the *maximum* (**5**) and *minimum* (**6**) level for each item of stock required by the organisation.

STATIONERY STOCK CARD

Item A4 Bond Paper (1) | Maximum level 50 (5) | Bin No 100

Minimum level 10 (6)

Unit Ream | Reorder level 20 (7)

Date	Receipts (2)			Issues (3)			Balance in stock (4)
	Qty	Inv no	Supplier	Qty	Req no	Dept	
199-							26
Jan 1							26
3				6	141	Accounts	20
4	30	A133	J Smith & Co				50
10				3	159	Personnel	47

Fig 5.2 A stock card

The stock record card also indicates the *reorder level* (**7**), which shows the stock level (quantity of stock) at which an order needs to be requested so that delivery is made before the remaining stock runs out. It is at this point that a **purchase requisition** is sent to the purchasing department (the buying department) to instruct the buyer to order the stock.

A stock record card will be kept for every item of stock and will therefore provide an up-to-date record of issues and requisitions, reorder levels, and the maximum and minimum amounts of stock required for any one particular organisation, department or office. The reorder level will take into account how long it takes for orders to be delivered together with the 'usage' level for that particular item.

You would expect to order regularly those items that have a high usage level because these are used more frequently. For example, A4 bond typing paper would be used daily in an office and you would need to keep up a regular supply. Whereas staplers, although used daily, are long lasting and their usage level would be very low, so that you would find you very seldom reorder these.

■ DIY 5.1.5

Look at the example of a stock record card in Fig 5.3. Notice that the columns give details of date, quantity received from supplier, invoice number, name of supplier, quantity issued to the individual departments, number of the requisition form, name of the department and the total balance left in stock. Colour coding can also be used to help you to identify a particular type of stock. For example, all stationery records may be on green cards, and manufacturing on yellow cards.

Anything coming into the organisation will be shown under the heading **Receipts**, and anything going out of the stockroom will be shown under the heading **Issues**. You may have already noticed that in this example the maximum stock level is shown as 800 reams, the minimum as 250 reams and the reorder level as 350 reams. A ream of paper is 500 sheets.

As you can see, this stock record card is incomplete, because the figures have not been added to or deducted from the total. Please copy the card on to a piece of paper and fill in the missing details.

STATIONERY STOCK CARD

Item Photocopying Paper, White | Maximum level 800 | Bin No 92

Unit Reams | Minimum level 250

Reorder level 350

Date	Receipts			Issues			Balance in stock
	Qty no	Inv	Supplier	Qty no	Req	Dept	
May 1							450
5				50	S101	Sales	
10				75	A199	Accounts	
11				75	P123	Personnel	
14	200	M21	Mason Ltd				
14				20	S102	Sales	

Fig 5.3 Stock record card (incomplete)

It is important that your calculations are correct. If they are not, you may find yourself in trouble for ordering stock that is not required or even worse, not ordering stock that is required. Imagine how you would feel if someone found that the organisation had run out of A4 typing paper but had 20 staplers in stock!

DIY 5.1.6

The stock record card shown in Fig 5.4 overleaf has been completed incorrectly. It is important to any organisation that mistakes are not made. Please check this card and copy the outline on to a piece of paper. Then rewrite the card and make the necessary amendments.

► *How is the stock ordered within an organisation?*

You should now be familiar with the sequence of events leading up to the delivery of goods to an organisation, and how such a delivery is

STATIONERY STOCK CARD

Item Envelopes, DL, White — Maximum level 100 — Bin No 12

Minimum level 20

Unit 50s — Reorder level 30

Date	Receipts			Issues			Balance in stock
	Qty	Inv no	Supplier	Qty	Req no	Dept	
Sept 1							40
Sept 9				3	P109	Production	36
Sept 10				6	A115	Accounts	30
Sept 10	30	J/42	Papermills plc				
Sept 14				4	S114	Sales	34
Sept 15				10	R102	Repro	44

Fig 5.4 Stock record card

recorded on the stock record card. However, as a member of an organisation, you will need to be aware of the procedures required in order to request supplies for your own working area.

Most organisations use **stock requisition forms** which are completed by the person needing the stock. These forms are usually countersigned by the supervisor and then passed over to the Stock Controller, who will arrange for the items to be taken from the stockroom.

If the Stock Controller identifies that stock is low and needs to be reordered from the supplier, then a **purchase requisition** would be sent to the purchasing, or buying, department to inform them that the minimum stock level had been reached and that new stock should be ordered immediately. It is the responsibility of the purchasing department to ensure that the stock is ordered, and also that the correct quality has been ordered at the best possible price.

Remember that every time stock is issued to a department it should be *deducted* from the stock record card, and every time stock is delivered by a supplier this should be *added* to the record card. The Stocktaker is employed to check the figures of stock received against stock issued to departments or sold to purchasers throughout the organisation, in order to calculate the total value of stock in hand and discover any mistakes.

You will find that the stock you are most likely to be called upon to order frequently in an office will be stationery. Stationery is classified as a consumable item of stock and is used in the administration of the organisation. It may be kept in the General Office, with a member of the office staff being responsible for it.

Items of stationery could include paper, envelopes, typewriter ribbons and lift-off tapes, paperclips, pencils, glue, pens, and so on. The value of this type of stock is very high and great care must be taken to control its use and ensure that staff are not requesting it for personal use, or storing unnecessary quantities.

■ DIY 5.1.7

You will see in Fig 5.5 a stationery requisition form that needs to be completed in order to top-up the existing stock in your office. You require 2 reams of A4

STATIONERY REQUISITION

No ....

Date ....

Quantity	Description

Signed ....

Department ....

Authorised ....

Storekeeper's initials

....

Fig 5.5 Stationery requisition form

paper (white), 1 ream of A4 paper (yellow), 2 boxes of C6 brown envelopes, 3 typewriter cartridges (carbon), 7 lift-off tapes and 2 each of blue, black and red felt-tip pens.

Copy the form on to a sheet of paper and fill in the required information. Remember to date the form and sign it. The next requisition number for your department is 201.

► *How is stock stored?*

You should now be aware that stock is a valuable asset to the organisation and must be kept in perfect condition. The type of storage required will depend upon the kind of stock and the size of the organisation. Large organisations will have a stockroom or department with staff employed to take charge of the stock; whereas a small organisation may have a stock cupboard with only one person in charge of the keys. What you must remember is that, however large or small the organisation, it is essential that the stock is stored correctly.

Every item of stock must be stored neatly and be easily accessible when required. Shelves should be labelled so that it is easy to find what is needed, and the stockroom or cupboard should always be kept locked. It is important that the stockroom or cupboard is kept dry at all times to prevent paper-based stock from becoming damp and going mouldy. Large or heavy items should be kept low down and, when new stock arrives, it should be placed at the back or at the bottom of the existing supply so that older stock is used first.

It is important that you treat hazardous stock with care. Any liquids that are dangerous or inflammable, for example thinners, glue or duplicating fluid, must be kept in a separate area, and staff must never smoke in this area or in the stockroom itself.

■ DIY 5.1.8

You are in charge of the General Office's stock cupboard and have decided that it could be better organised. Here is a list of the items that are kept in the cupboard. You have to decide whether you are going to place them on a shelf at the top, middle or bottom of the cupboard. Make three lists under the headings of top, middle or bottom, and identify the items you would place in each position by using their stock number.

Items	Stock number
10 reams A4 Typing paper (white)	PA4W
1 gallon Duplicating Fluid	DF1
20 reams A4 Typing paper (headed)	PA4H
4 staplers	ST10
10 boxes staples	ST5
2 boxes A4 carbon paper	CP06
1 ream A3 red poster paper	PA3PR
1 large box photocopier toner	PCT041
2 small boxes elastic bands	EBS2
1 ream A3 white card	PA3CW
10 red pens	RP1
5 reams A4 Typing paper (yellow)	PA4Y
20 Typewriter cartridges	TWCB1
5 small boxes paperclips	PCS1
1 typewriter	TWE1065
45 blue pens	BP1
1 ink duplicator	IDE1066
1 litre glue	1LG

▶ *How are stock levels checked?*

Stock levels are checked at regular intervals by a process called **stocktaking** or **reconciliation**. This means that every item of stock in the organisation is counted to calculate how much money is tied up in the value of the stock. This stocktaking produces a document called an **inventory**. It is the stocktaker's job to check that the balances of stock shown on the record cards are the same as the amount of stock actually in the stockroom; and that every issue of stock has a requisition form to support it – if it does not, then this means that the stock has been taken without authority.

■ DIY 5.1.9

In order to understand how a stock inventory is carried out, now is a good time to have a go yourself. Prepare a simple stock inventory sheet using the same layout as shown below. Carry out a stock check on three separate days – a

STOCK INVENTORY RECORD SHEET				
STOCK		QUANTITY		
Description	Unit	Date	Date	Date

Fig 5.6 Stock inventory record sheet

small stationery cupboard is sufficient for this task. When you have finished the third stocktake, your final set of figures, added to the stock taken figures (detailed on the requisition forms) should total the amount of stock which you started with. If it is less, this would show that somebody is taking stationery without completing a requisition form!

It is possible to keep an up-to-date record of stock levels by using a computer, which is what is done by the bar code reading tills you see in supermarkets. The computer will deduct from the total stock level every time some item of stock is taken out, and add to the stock level every time stock is replaced. This is a very good method of keeping a check of the stock, but one disadvantage is that the figures it gives you are those that it has calculated to be correct. It cannot take into account theft, pilfering, damage, loss, etc, unless these details are fed into it.

Therefore, you will find that manual stocktaking still has to take place at least once a year so that the actual value of stock can be entered into the organisation's annual accounts sheet. It is during this stock-take that damaged stock, or perhaps stock which has become obsolete (out of date) and is no longer required, can be 'written off' and its value deducted from the organisation's assets. Some organisations will have a sale to reduce the amount of 'written off' stock which they hold.

You should now be aware of the type of stock you are likely to find in any organisation. You also know that consumable items, such as stationery, are used in the administration of the business. Whether you work in a large or small organisation, it is of great importance that stock is stored correctly, especially hazardous stock. A regular check should be made to find out current stock levels and to indicate any loss or damage.

■ DIY 5.1.10

Copy out the following information. The paragraphs have been started for you, but you will need to complete them.

1. Consumables are supplies which are used in the administration and smooth running of the organisation. They are used quickly and need to be ordered regularly. Four examples of consumable items are ...
2. An example of consumable supplies would be stationery. Twelve items of stationery I would expect to find in a stock cupboard would be ....
3. Some supplies need to be reordered regularly as they are used often, whereas other supplies would be ordered on demand. Three examples of supplies that would be required on a regular basis are... Three examples of supplies that would be ordered on demand are ...
4. When storing paper-based materials it is important to ...
5. Hazardous materials should be stored ...
6. A storeroom should ...
7. It is important to keep the storeroom locked because ...
8. It is necessary to do physical stock checks at least once a year because... This is called a ... or ...
9. Computers can be used to help in finding stock levels but the disadvantage of this is ...
10. If I were in charge of the stock cupboard I would always ...

► *What legislation is there relating to the receipt of goods?*

When you or your organisation buys goods or services, you are called a 'consumer'. Did you know that there are a number of 'consumer laws' to protect you? Possible dangers that may be encountered are:

- misleading advertisements
- dangerous goods
- incorrect description of goods
- incorrect weight or size
- goods not suitable for their purpose
- goods paid for but not delivered
- poor quality, making goods unusable
- incorrect price information giving idea of a bargain
- businesses getting together to keep prices high
- credit terms not showing exactly how much you pay
- persuasive or pressurised buying that you later regret

There are a variety of organisations set up to give advice and provide consumer protection. These include the British Standards Institute (BSI), the Consumers' Association and the Citizens Advice Bureau. However, as a consumer, you are also protected by law – this protection is in the form of a number of 'consumer laws'.

Sale of Goods Act 1979

This Act sets out the conditions under which goods can be bought and sold. The goods must:

- be legally owned by the seller
- suit the purpose for which they are sold
- fit their description
- correspond with samples
- be capable of use for the purpose intended

The buyer has the right to return the goods and have the money refunded, or to claim compensation, depending on the particular breach of law involved.

If someone tried to sell you 'Big Ben', or wellington boots which let in the water, or A3 paper instead of A4, then they would be in breach of this law and you could take legal action.

Weights and Measures Acts 1963 to 1979

These Acts make it an offence to give a short (too little) weight or measure, even by accident. Local authorities employ trading standards officers to enforce these Acts, and as part of their work they regularly visit shops and other premises to check the accuracy of scales and other measuring devices used. As a consumer you would be protected when buying goods such as potatoes, petrol or a pint of beer in a pub.

Trade Descriptions Acts 1968 and 1972

It is an offence to describe goods or services for sale in a false or misleading way. This applies to verbal as well as written descriptions, and suppliers must ensure that advertisements do not contain wrong information about goods for sale.

As a consumer you must be told the origin of the goods, ie where they were made, together with the original price of an item which is now being offered at sale price.

Unsolicited Goods and Services Act 1971

This Act protects you if you are sent goods that you did not order. If you inform the supplier that you do not wish to keep the goods, it is the supplier's responsibility to collect these goods from you within 30 days or the goods become your property. Alternatively, you need do nothing other than to wait for six months, after which time the goods will also become your property.

Fair Trading Act 1973

This Act set up an Office of Fair Trading under a Director-General of Fair Trading. It has very wide responsibilities concerning unfair trading practices which affect consumers. It is the responsibility of the Office of Fair Trading to ensure that trade is carried out according to the law.

■ DIY 5.1.11

As a consumer, did you realise that you were protected so well? It is very important for you to know the consumer rights of both yourself and the organisation for which you work. However, it is an unfortunate fact that most people do not know their rights. Design a leaflet on a piece of folded A4 paper that explains, in simple terms, the rights of the consumer and where advice can be found.

Completing Unit 5

To complete this unit on stock control you will need to put all DIY tasks in your folder, and carry out a final assessment. The assessment must cover a two-month period of keeping stock records and an inventory.

If you are responsible at work for stocktaking, you will be able to get credit by showing your tutor or assessor what you do. The records must still cover a two-month period and an inventory reconciliation – a one-day visit to the stockroom or stock controller is not enough.

Claiming credit

Once you have completed your final assessment you will need to write in your record book or folder *how, when, where* and *what* you have done to prove that you are competent.

The following is an example of how one trainee completed this claim:

5.1.a While on work experience at Coopers and Co, from 5.5.9– to 23.5.9–, I ensured that stock requisitions were completed accurately and delivered to staff as soon as possible.

5.1.b I always made sure that stock was stored safely and securely, and that hazardous items (thinners) were kept in a separate place.

5.1.c I carried out stock checks on the stationery cupboard over a two-month period. I completed one inventory reconciliation and reported shortages and damaged items to my supervisor.

5.1.d When I received incoming deliveries these were checked against the delivery note. The delivery note was checked against the original order and any mistakes were reported to my supervisor.

5.1.e I recorded incoming and outgoing stock neatly and accurately on stock record cards.

UNIT 6
Mail handling

Element 6.1
RECEIVE, SORT AND DISTRIBUTE INCOMING/ INTERNAL MAIL

Mail arriving at an organisation may include many different documents. There may be letters, quotations, orders, invoices, enquiries, applications for jobs and advertising material sent by other organisations. It is very important to open and distribute the mail to each department without delay, so that office staff are able to make a start on their day's work as soon as they arrive in the office.

In a large organisation, it is usual practice for mailroom staff to start work before the other office workers in order to make sure that all the mail has been delivered to each department by the time the office workers are ready to begin their day. However, in a small office it may the case that only one person is responsible for opening, sorting and delivering the mail.

Some organisations rent a private box or bag from the Post Office for an annual fee. This allows the organisation to collect mail or parcels from the Post Office every day, except Sunday. The organisation can collect mail from their box or bag early in the morning to ensure that it has been sorted and delivered to each department ready for action at the beginning of the day. If an organisation has no private box or bag at the Post Office's delivery office, mail will be delivered in the normal way.

▶ *How should incoming mail be sorted?*

Each organisation will have its own procedure for dealing with incoming mail, depending on size and type of business carried out. For example, a large mail order company would employ experienced staff working to a strict timetable, who are able to use specialist equipment. A smaller company may only employ one person who deals with mail as one of a number of responsibilities and, therefore, follows a less rigid timetable.

In both cases remember that all mail is important, regardless of the size of the organisation. Mail which fails to reach its destination quickly and accurately may result in the loss of valuable business.

▶ *How do most organisations deal with incoming mail?*

These are the steps which are likely to be followed:

1 Sign for registered and recorded delivery items. (Details of these may have to be entered into a Special Mail Register.)

SPECIAL MAIL REGISTER				
Date	Time	Sender	Method of Delivery	Received By

Fig 6.1 Special mail register

■ DIY 6.1.1

Make your own copy of a page from a Special Mail Register. Enter the following details of post received by you at 9.00 am today:

- Recorded delivery letter from J R Nesbitt & Co
- Recorded delivery packet from T Blake & Associates

- Registered letter from Mr J D Duncan
- Recorded delivery packet from Howells
- Trackback parcel from Office Supplies Ltd
- Datapost parcel from Consortium Limited

2 Remove all mail that is marked 'Private' or 'Confidential' and put it to one side.

3 Open envelopes, using a paper knife or your finger. Alternatively, a letter opening machine may be used, in which case the contents of the letter should first be 'tapped' down to the bottom of the envelope so they are not cut with the blade.

Do not open registered, recorded delivery, personal or confidential mail. This mail is usually taken for opening to the department or person to whom it is addressed.

4 Remove the contents carefully from each envelope, checking that nothing has been left inside. Attach all enclosures to the back of the letter with either a paperclip or staple. Enclosures are indicated at the bottom of the correspondence by the letters 'Enc' or 'Encs'. If the enclosure is not there, write 'NOT ENCLOSED' on the letter.

You or another member of staff will have the responsibility of contacting the sender of the letter to inform him/her of the missing enclosure.

5 Date stamp all the mail – in the case of mail which is registered, recorded delivery, private or confidential, date stamp the unopened envelope. (Some electric date stamps print the time as well as the date.)

6 Some organisations require a record of all incoming mail to be kept, usually in a special file or book. Most organisations will require mail that contains remittances in the form of cash, postal orders, stamps or cheques to be recorded in a Remittances Book. Each day details of remittances received are entered into the book. They are then totalled up and handed over to the Chief Cashier, who will sign the book, which acts as your receipt.

■ DIY 6.1.2

Make your own copy of a page from a Remittances Book. Enter the following

REMITTANCES BOOK				
Date	Sender	Type of Payment	Amount £	Signed

Fig 6.2 Remittances book

remittances that have been received by you today:

- Messrs Givens & Co enclosed a cheque for £26.97
- Mrs C Cuthbert enclosed a postal order for £2.30
- Mr J K King enclosed £45.00 in cash
- Long & Co enclosed a cheque for £109.45
- Natasha Vincent enclosed a postal order for £3.98
- Mrs T Forrest enclosed 72p in stamps

When you have entered all remittances, total the amount column.

7 Date stamp empty envelopes, as they may be needed at some future time to give details of when the letter was posted or indicate a return address. Some organisations reuse these envelopes for their own internal mail.

8 Sort mail. This can be done directly into pigeon-holes or wire trays labelled with details of departments or individual members of staff. Also sort internal mail into the correct pigeon-hole or tray. All mail will then be delivered, or await collection.

If the mail is not addressed to a particular department or person, look for a subject heading which may indicate where it has to go; or read through the letter to see if the contents give any clues. If you are still unsure, put the letter to one side and deal with it later. It is important not to hold up the rest of the mail while dealing with a query.

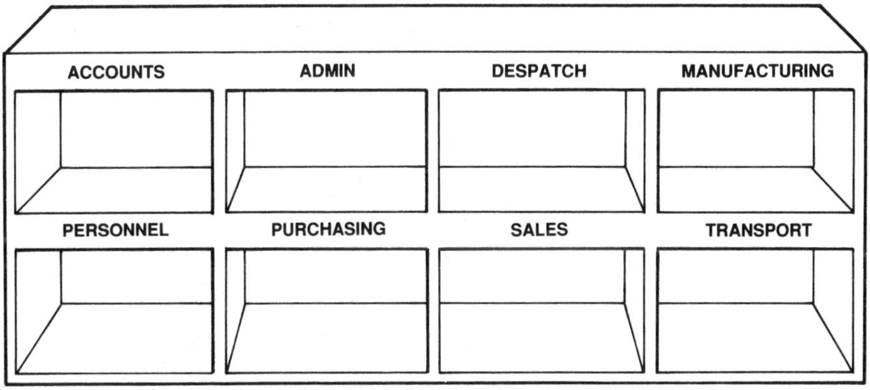

Fig 6.3 Pigeon-holes for mail

■ DIY 6.1.3

Copy the diagram in Fig 6.3 of mail pigeon-holes.

Here is a list of mail received today. Each item has a number which should be written into the correct department's pigeon-hole. If you have any uncertainties, place the number of the item below the pigeon-holes to indicate that you will sort this out later.

- Letter addressed to the Sales Manager (**1**)
- Leaflets regarding health and safety at work (**2**)
- Price list for new computers (**3**)
- Job enquiry (**4**)
- Letter addressed to Buying Manager (**5**)
- Request for a company price list (**6**)
- Time Sheets from Manchester Branch (**7**)
- Internal post for Ken Shaw in Despatch (**8**)
- Invoice for stationery (**9**)
- Registered letter for Manufacturing Manager (**10**)
- Final demand for telephone bill (**11**)
- Internal post for wages clerk (**12**)

9 If a piece of correspondence requires the attention of more than one person or department, either take the required number of photocopies and send one to each department/person concerned, or attach a circulation or routing slip (Fig 6.4) detailing the names of other people or departments who need to see it. Once the correspondence

ROUTING SLIP Read or copy and pass on in order shown below:		
Name	Department	Initial/Date
Please return to: By:		

Fig 6.4 Routing slip

has been seen by the named person they will cross their name from the list and then pass the correspondence on to the next person.

■ DIY 6.1.4

Make your own copy of a routing slip. You have received in today's post notification of the company's annual awards ceremony. To ensure all staff see the notice, complete your routing slip with the following information:

Mrs J B Shepherd, Head of Accounts
Ms N Dyer, Administration
Mr D F G Hays, Personnel Officer
Sally Richmond, Purchasing

You wish the original notice to be returned to you by Friday of next week.

10 Once the bulk of the mail has been sorted, go back and deal with any mail that was put to one side.

▶ *What should you do with damaged or suspicious items?*

When you collect or receive the daily mail, check to ensure there are no damaged items. If any items are damaged in any way there may be a Post Office label to confirm this was done during sorting. If there is no label, point out the damage to the delivery person or contact the local customer care department. The organisation may wish to claim compensation from the Post Office for the damage and can only do so if they have evidence that the item(s) were damaged before delivery or collection.

Always make sure you treat mail as instructed, if 'Handle with care', 'Do not bend' or 'Fragile' labels are stuck on to an item, treat it accordingly. Also look for pictures on packages, such as a broken glass, which indicates fragile contents, or an arrow which is used to show the correct way 'up'. If you do not obey these instructions and damage the item, it is your fault and the organisation cannot claim compensation from the Post Office.

If you are ever suspicious about a piece of mail then do not open, prod, shake or squeeze it. Your suspicions may be aroused if the item has an unusual smell (some explosives smell of marzipan!); if it is of an unusual shape or size; and if it has strange writing, spelling or wrapping – in fact, anything that is 'out of the ordinary' should make you suspicious.

If you are suspicious of an item, the first thing you should always do is to tell your supervisor. Your supervisor will then be able to contact the department or person to whom the item is addressed and ask if they are expecting such a package. If the package has a return address, this can be contacted to confirm the contents of the package. However, if there is no such address and your own staff are unaware of the delivery of such a package, then it is wise for all personnel to leave the office, lock the door and contact either security or the police.

Large organisations often use machinery that can scan mail, in the same way as luggage is scanned at airports. Mail and packages can be passed through a type of X-ray machine that produces an image of their contents on a screen. Staff are trained to recognise suspicious contents and to know the procedures to be taken if their suspicions are aroused.

Remember that 'suspicious' does not always mean a letter bomb.

Individual staff may be 'under attack' for personal reasons or the organisation itself may be open to attack because of the nature of the work it carries out. Security procedures for mail should never be taken lightly – if you work in a government department dealing with sensitive information, or for a fur coat manufacturer, or perhaps a cosmetics company which carries out testing on animals, you would have to take security very seriously!

Remember, if you are ever in doubt, tell your supervisor immediately.

▶ *What should you do if unable to deliver mail on time?*

There will always be times when things just do not go smoothly and you may find yourself unable to deliver the mail on time. If this happens, it is essential that you tell your supervisor immediately. It is only then that something can be done to help you out – if your supervisor is unaware of the problem, you will not be able to get help!

It is important for you to remember that your work colleagues will be organising their day according to priorities, some of which will be affected by what is in the daily mail. Therefore, one of your own priorities will be to ensure that your colleagues get their mail as early as possible.

If for any reason you are unable to do this, you should always look to see if any of the day's mail is marked 'Urgent'. If it is, make sure this is delivered immediately with an explanation that the rest of the mail will follow later. You should encourage colleagues to let you know if they are expecting an urgent delivery so that you can make sure it is delivered to them as soon as it arrives on your desk.

■ DIY 6.1.5

Complete the following sentences. Try to write as much as you can to prove you understand what to do.

1 If I received damaged mail I would ...
2 If I received a suspicious package I would not ...
3 If I received a suspicious package I would ...
4 If I was unable to deliver mail on time I would ...
5 If I received urgent mail I would make sure it was ...

Completing Element 6.1

To complete this element on incoming mail you will need to put all DIY tasks in your folder and carry out a final assessment. This assessment must include the sorting and delivery of a minimum of 10 consecutive mail items over three separate occasions.

If you are responsible for incoming mail at work, you will be able to get credit for this by showing your tutor or assessor what you do. For this you will need to complete a log over a period of time, detailing all your incoming mail activities.

Claiming credit

Once you have completed your final assessment, you will need to write in your record book or folder *how, when, where* and *what* you have done to prove that you are competent.

The following is an example of how one trainee completed this claim:

6.1.a While on work placement at Coopers and Co, from 5.5.9–to 23.5.9–, I did not receive any damaged or suspicious mail. If I had, I would have reported this to my supervisor immediately.

6.1.b I checked all enclosures and stapled them to the document. If there had been any missing enclosures, I would have told my supervisor immediately.

6.1.c I made sure that any cash or valuables were delivered to the correct person immediately. I did not use a remittances book, but covered this in an assignment (see work folder).

6.1.d I used a paper knife to open the mail. I made sure the contents were not damaged.

6.1.e I used pigeon-holes to sort mail into departments. I delivered the mail to the correct department or person as early as possible.

6.1.f During my work experience I did not have any unavoidable delays, but if I had, I would have told my supervisor immediately in order to make sure that all urgent mail was delivered.

■ Element 6.2

PREPARE FOR DESPATCH OUTGOING/INTERNAL MAIL

If you are given the responsibility of dealing with the despatch of mail, you must have a thorough knowledge of the Post Office mail service and its regulations. Mail services are also offered by other organisations such as Securicor, DHS, TNT and Group 4 – you will find other delivery companies detailed in *Yellow Pages*.

▶ *The Post Office*

The Post Office Corporation is now made up of three separate businesses: Royal Mail, Parcelforce and Post Office Counters Ltd.

Royal Mail is responsible for the collection and delivery of nearly 60 million items a day to 24 million addresses nationwide. It provides a wide range of special services designed to cater for businesses and private mail users. Royal Mail uses a two-tier system of service for postal delivery.

▶ *What is the two-tier postal system?*

The Post Office offers a two-tier system for the delivery of letters (parcel post is just a one-tier service). First-class post costs more but arrives at its destination within about 24 hours. Second-class post is cheaper but slower, although post should be delivered by the third working day. When preparing mail for despatch it is important to consider costs, and so mail should be sorted and stamped according to its urgency. It is pointless sending mail by first class if it is not urgently required, as this will only have the effect of increasing the company's postage costs.

Parcelforce provides a nationwide parcel delivery service. It offers a variety of services for business and private users, including Datapost.

Post Office Counters Ltd operates as an agent for many of the services offered by Royal Mail and Parcelforce through its network of 20,000 post offices across the country – over 1,000 main post offices and over 19,000 owned and run by agents. You can use the post office for:

- Girobank and cash dispensers
- Pension, child benefit and other allowances
- TV and motor vehicle licences
- Payment of bills over the counter such as gas, electricity, telephone and water rates
- National Savings Premium and Government Bonds, Ordinary and

Investment Savings Accounts, and Savings Certificates
- British Visitor's Passport and excursion documents
- Payment of Council tax
- Postal Orders
- Photobooths
- Stamp and coin collections
- Telepoint, telephone cards and Mercuryphones

▶ *What Post Office services are available?*

The Post Office publishes a *Mail Guide* which gives details of all regulations, services and costs. The *Mail Guide*, costs approximately £20. You may find a copy in the library or your place of work. It should be updated regularly in accordance with new literature despatched by the Post Office. There are, however, many leaflets available from the Post Office that will give you up-to-date information and prices on most of their services. Remember that if you are unsure of what service to use for a particular item, post office counter staff are there to help you and will give advice.

However, it is important to remember that the Post Office offers many services in competition with private companies. Therefore, costs may vary considerably and will need to be taken into account when selecting the most appropriate service.

■ DIY 6.2.1

Call in to your local post office and collect as many leaflets as you can on postal services and rates. Particularly useful leaflets are: *UK Letter Rates – A Comprehensive Guide; International Letter Rates - A Comprehensive Guide; Wrap up Well; Parcelforce Standard; Parcelforce International; and Parcelforce Datapost.*

Also collect an example of a Royal Mail Special Delivery label, a Recorded Delivery label and a Certificate of Posting. Place all the leaflets, labels, etc, in a safe place – you will need to refer to them later on.

Some of the more frequently used services are as follows:

Certificate of posting

This is the cheapest way of making sure that an inland ordinary letter or parcel, or overseas ordinary letters have actually been posted. It gives the sender proof of posting and compensation can be claimed from the Post Office for loss or damage. The letter or parcel has to be handed in at a Post Office for the counter clerk to complete and stamp a receipt. Delivery is made in the normal way and the item does not have to be signed for by the recipient. Compensation will not be paid if money or jewellery is sent in the ordinary post, even if covered by a certificate of posting.

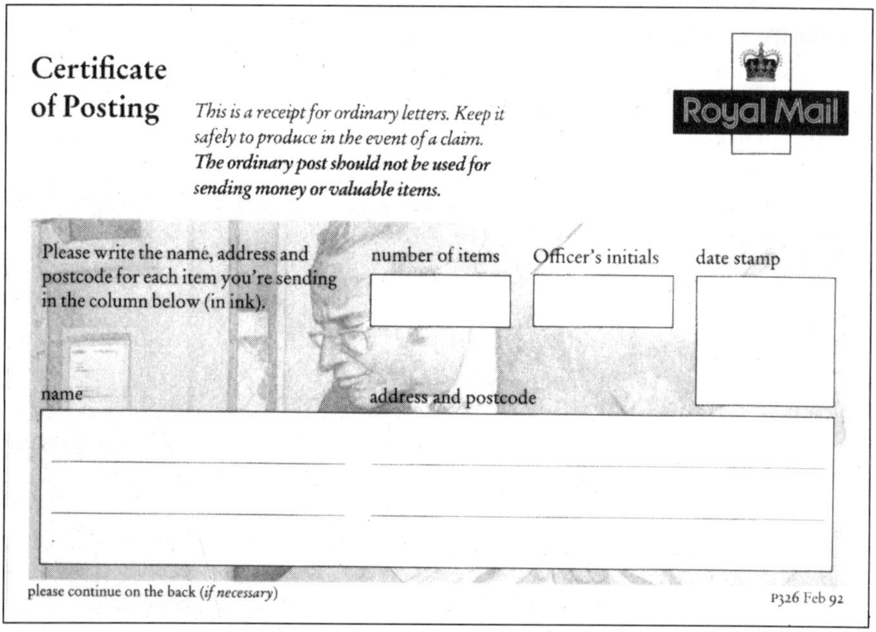

Certificate of Posting

This is a receipt for ordinary letters. Keep it safely to produce in the event of a claim.
The ordinary post should not be used for sending money or valuable items.

Royal Mail

Please write the name, address and postcode for each item you're sending in the column below (in ink).

number of items

Officer's initials

date stamp

name

address and postcode

please continue on the back (*if necessary*)

P326 Feb 92

Fig 6.5 Certificate of Posting

Recorded delivery – first- and second-class mail

This service provides a certificate of posting and a signature from the recipient to confirm delivery. It can be used for important documents, such as passports, examination certificates and legal documents. Limited compensation will be paid for loss or damage but this is only to cover for the inconvenience caused. Therefore, this service is not suitable for money or jewellery. Stickers provided by the Post Office for this service are bright orange in colour and have an identification number.

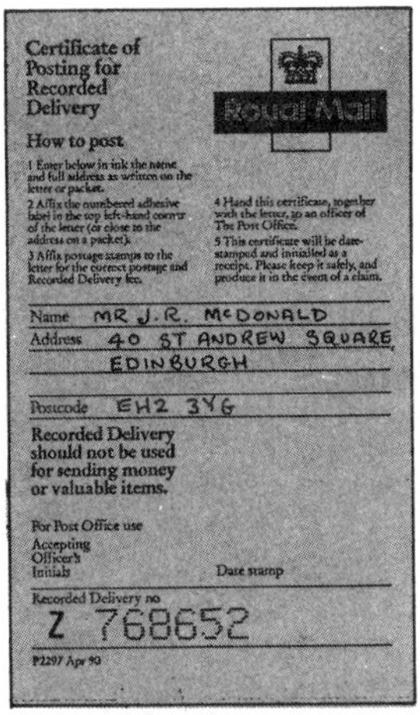

Fig 6.6 Recorded delivery slip

Registered post – first-class mail only

If you wish to send anything valuable in the post, such as cash or jewellery, you should use this service. The fee you pay will depend on the value of the item being sent. If the item is lost or damaged, compensation will be paid according to its value. This service provides you with a certificate of posting and the signature of the recipient when the post is delivered. Letters and packets sent by registered post are handled with special security measures and kept separate from ordinary mail. Special registered envelopes can be bought from the Post Office which have two blue lines across each side and these must be used if sending cash.

Fig 6.7 Envelope for registered post

Royal Mail special delivery

This service is for first-class mail only and can be used for letters and parcels. It offers extra assurance that the mail will arrive the next working day after posting. The words 'Special Delivery' must be marked above the address on the left-hand side of the letter or parcel, and a broad blue or black line must be drawn from top to bottom on front and back of a letter, and completely round a parcel. This service will deliver the mail by messenger after its arrival at the office of delivery, provided that this will ensure earlier delivery than by normal postal treatment.

Datapost

This service provides delivery of urgent letters, packets and parcels by no later than 12.00 noon the next day. It guarantees overnight delivery within the United Kingdom and speedy delivery to many overseas countries. If an item is not delivered on time, compensation can be claimed from the Post Office. If Datapost is to be used regularly, the Post Office will arrange a regular contract.

Swiftair

Swiftair is an express airmail service available at an extra fee for all letters to Europe, and for letters and printed papers to most other countries. The item is moved as fast as possible within the UK and receives express delivery abroad in those countries where this is available. A certificate of posting can also be obtained, although a particular delivery time cannot be guaranteed.

Fig 6.8 Swiftair

FreePost

This service allows people to send mail free of charge to an organisation. The Post Office issues the organisation with a licence to operate a FreePost service, and the word 'FREEPOST' can then be included in the address. The service requires no special stationery, unless first-class service is required, and it allows customers sending orders to a company, for example, to do this without having to pay postage. FreePost is often used to encourage people to reply to advertisements, and you may have seen it used in magazines or on television.

■ DIY 6.2.2

Your supervisor has asked you to recommend the most suitable postal service for the following items. Choose which you think would be the best from the services already explained above.

1 A packet containing £200 in cash
2 A letter confirming the receipt of a complaint
3 A gold bracelet
4 A passport
5 An important contract that has to be in Edinburgh by tomorrow
6 A letter to Paris inviting someone to an interview this week
7 A sales campaign in a national magazine for the company's new products

▶ *How can you help the Post Office?*

First, always make sure you put the right postage on all items. Post Office charges are calculated on the service required, the urgency of delivery, the destination and weight of an item. Up-to-date charges can be found in Post Office leaflets, both national and international, which should be used at all times to ensure correct postage is paid. If too little has been paid, the person receiving the item of mail will be asked by the Post Office to pay double the missing amount!

Always use standard size envelopes. The Post Office uses machinery that handles and sorts mail automatically and asks its customers to use envelope sizes that are 'post office preferred' – known as POP. You should use envelopes no smaller than 90 mm x 140 mm, and no larger

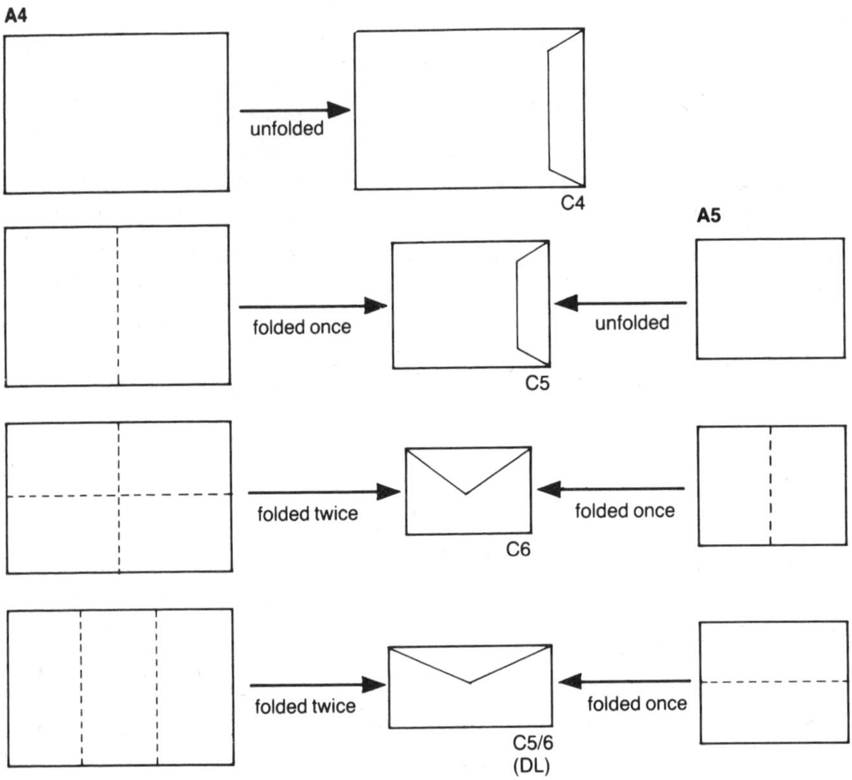

Fig 6.9 Envelope sizes

than 120 mm x 235 mm. Envelopes should be oblong in shape, made of paper weighing at least 63 gsm (grammes per square metre) and no thicker than 6 mm, including their contents. The most commonly-used envelopes are **DL** (110 mm x 220 mm), **C 6** (114 mm x 162 mm), **C 5** (162 mm x 229 mm) and **C 4** (229 mm x 324 mm).

■ DIY 6.2.3

Collect an example of each of the four most commonly-used sizes of envelope and write on each the correct reference number. Stick each envelope on to a piece of A4 paper, and underneath each envelope explain in words, or by using diagrams, how a piece of A4 paper would be folded to fit into that envelope. Also find an example of a window envelope, fold a piece of A4 paper to fit into this, and place your own address in the correct place so it shows through the window.

Note: If you have already completed Unit 3 task DIY 3.1.2, you will not have to do this DIY task. Make a note about this on a piece of paper and insert it into your folder for Unit 6 as evidence.

Regardless of the service used, it is vitally important to address all mail legibly and always to use the postcode. Labels for envelopes should be typed or produced on a word processor. If you have to write envelopes, make sure your writing is 'readable'. Always write the town in capitals, and put the postcode on a separate line. If you cannot fit the postcode on a separate line, leave about five character spaces after the town and put it there.

In order to help the Post Office to sort mail quickly and efficiently, postcodes are used to identify the exact location of the addressee. Post Office sorting staff are able to key in the postcode using electronic keyboarding equipment that marks the envelope with a series of dots. Automated sorting equipment can read these dots and will divert the mail to the correct location according to the area indicated by the postcode.

Therefore, if you use the correct postal address and full postcode on all items, you will help to ensure quick and accurate delivery. If you are not sure of a full address or postcode, ask your local Postal Customer Care Unit (you can find the number in the *Phone Book* and in the *Mail Guide*).

▶ *What items must not be sent through the post?*

Dangerous items and substances should not be sent through the post nationally or internationally. The *Mail Guide* provides a list of items and substances, such as aerosols, lighters, asbestos, enamels, varnishes, explosives and prohibited drugs, which should never be sent by post. Live creatures, such as bees, leeches and worms, can be sent by post provided they are sent first-class in adequate packing, but creatures such as poisonous spiders cannot be sent!

Mr J L Protheroe
Mobley & Co Ltd
1 Somerly Close
COVENTRY
CV3 2LA

Fig 6.10

▶ *How should an envelope be addressed?*

Most organisations use a blocked style for addresses on envelopes. The address may be typed directly on to the envelope, or sticky labels can be used which can be peeled from their backing and placed in the correct position on the envelope.

The address should be placed half-way down the envelope and a third of the way in from the left-hand side. Remember to leave enough space for the envelope to be franked across the top and, if stamps are used, the Post Office will need to cancel these out with an ink impression. If you have placed the address too high, the top half of the address may become unreadable!

If the letter is confidential, private or has a 'For the attention of' line,

FOR THE ATTENTION OF
MR J L PROTHEROE

Mobley & Co Ltd
1 Somerly Close
COVENTRY
CV3 2LA

Fig 6.11

this should be placed one clear line space above the address in capitals.

Note that on both examples the town has been typed in capitals and the postcode placed on a line of its own. If any special instructions are included (for example, CONFIDENTIAL or PRIVATE), these should always be typed in capitals and/or underlined. Special instructions such as 'DO NOT BEND' or a postal label such as 'RECORDED DELIVERY' should be placed on the top left-hand corner of the envelope – remember that the stamp is placed on the right-hand corner.

Some organisations require staff to mark envelopes with a pencilled '1' or '2' in the top right-hand corner of the envelope to indicate to mail-room staff whether first-class or second-class postage is required. However, if the envelope is to be delivered by hand and requires no postage, it is usual to type or write 'BY HAND' in the top right-hand corner of the envelope.

■ DIY 6.2.4

Prepare envelopes or paper, cut to DL size, for each of the following mail items:

1. Darby & Son, 12 Old Lane, Brighton, BR9 7HT
   For the attention of Ms L K Patel
2. Mr R Jones, 342 Link Lane, Bradford-on-Avon, Wilts, BA3 8YU Confidential
3. Messrs Kane & Cameron, Solicitors, 45 The Avenue, Frome, BA4 2FR
4. Miss S Perri, 67 Hazel Street, Comrie, Perth, EB4 8TU Private
5. Ms A Handrick, Malzstr 60 PSF 207, 0-2000 Neubrandenberg, Germany
6. Internal Mail, Personnel Department, Newcastle Branch By hand

▶ *How should mail be prepared?*

All items for mailing should be securely sealed in appropriate sized envelopes, packets or parcels. Mail should be legibly addressed and the correct postal rates should be calculated and applied. Post Office sorting requirements should also be followed. You will find that each organisation has its own procedure for preparing outgoing mail, and it is important for you to ensure that you know this procedure so that mistakes are not made.

If an organisation is large enough to have its own mailroom, there will be a system of regular collection of mail from every department during the day. Trays marked 'outgoing mail' are usually placed in each department so that mail can be collected and prepared during periods of the day when the mailroom is not so busy. The mailroom will probably advise staff of a final collection time, after which no mail will be accepted for that day. This will avoid a last-minute rush and ensure that Post Office collection times can be met.

In the case of bulky envelopes, these will have to be weighed and the correct postage calculated. The job of putting the contents into their envelopes may be done by the members of staff who typed/keyed in or wrote them, or it may be done by staff in the mailroom itself.

The procedure for this outgoing mail should be as follows:

1 Check the bottom of the letter for 'Enc'. If the enclosure is not there, put the letter to one side while you prepare the other mail.

2 Check that the letter has been signed.

3 Check that the inside address is the same as the address on the envelope.

4 If the letter is marked 'Confidential' or 'Private', make sure the envelope is too. Also check that 'For the attention of' information has also been included on the envelope.

5 Fold the letter so that it is creased as few times as possible. DL size envelopes are normally used, which require A4 paper to be folded

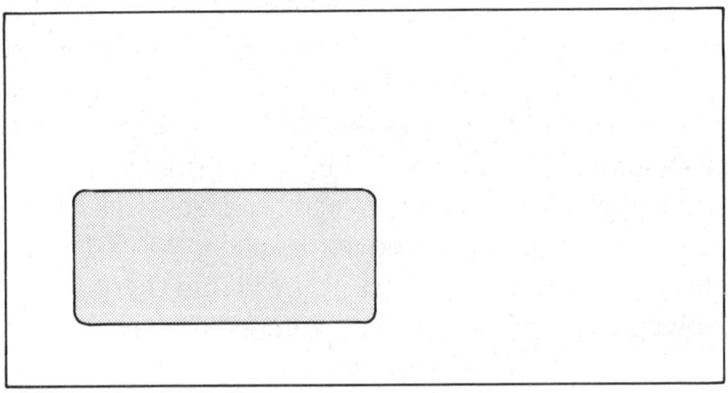

Fig 6.12 A window envelope

twice into three equal sections. A4 paper can also be left flat and placed into a C4 envelope, or folded in half and placed into a C5 envelope, or folded in half again to fit into a C6 envelope.

If window envelopes are used, check that the address on the letter can be read through the window. Some organisations mark their headed paper with a small box into which the address should be typed and/or mark the edges of the paper to show where the letter should be folded. This ensures the address is in the correct place to be seen through the window in the envelope.

6 If the letter is bulky or addressed to a country overseas, it may need extra postage. The correct postage can be calculated by weighing the item on a set of scales and then looking up the weight in the *Post Office Rates* leaflet.

7 Affix the correct stamps and place the letter into one of the following three categories:

- First class
- Second class
- Registered post/Recorded Delivery – taken to Post Office as a receipt has to be obtained.

Fig 6.13 Electronic scales for weighing post

If the mail has been prepared using a franking machine, all first-class items should be placed in a red post office bag and second-class items in a green post office bag.

The mail is now ready to be collected by or delivered to the Post Office. Remember that there will be a cut-off time in the afternoon, usually around 1700 hours, after which the Post Office will not accept post for that day.

■ DIY 6.2.5

Prepare for despatch the envelopes completed in task DIY 6.2.4. Write in pencil in the top right-hand corner of each envelope the correct postage required or, if possible, use a franking machine to frank each envelope ready for despatch. Match the item number given in DIY 6.2.4 for each envelope to tell you the service required.

1 Recorded delivery, first class
2 Second class
3 Recorded delivery, second class
4 First class
5 Swiftair
6 By hand

Calculate how much it would cost to send one packet to:

- Germany weighing 65 g
- France weighing 45 g
- Australia weighing 75 g using Airmail

8 Once the mail is prepared, go back to any items that were put to one side. You will have to inform the person responsible for the correspondence of the reason why it has missed the post. Remember that it is not your fault if he/she has forgotten to sign the letter or perhaps left out the enclosure. However, do try to inform them of the problem as soon as you can so that it can be put right, if possible in enough time to catch the afternoon's outgoing mail.

9 If stamps have been used for the mail, complete the Postage Book. This book gives a detailed record of all letters, packages and parcels posted. It also keeps a check on how many postage stamps have been used. Remember that stamps cost money and are not for private use.

POSTAGE BOOK			
Stamps Bought	Name and Town of Addressee	Stamps Used	Special Services
£20.00	2.7.9–	£ p	
	J Jones – Derby	0.48	
	S Ferry – Cardiff	0.97	Reg Mail
	Messrs Pike & Co – Hull	7.40	Parcel
	Smith & Son – London	0.54	Rec Del
	TOTAL	£9.39	
	Balance c/f	£10.61	
		£20.00	

Fig 6.14 Postage book

Therefore, a receipt (in other words some form of postage record) is completed to identify how the stamps have been used. The Postage Book and the stamps themselves should always be kept safe and secure, usually under lock and key to prevent dishonest use.

■ DIY 6.2.6

Copy a page from a Postage Book. Enter the following details:

Stamps bought today: £12.00

First-class letters to:
R Foster, Coventry
P B Associates, Newcastle
Lapper & Co, London

Second-class letters to:
J R Penfold, Glasgow
Data Protection Registrar, London

Recorded delivery to:
Derby & Sons, Brighton (first class)
Kane & Cameron, Frome (second class)

Airmail to:

K Roo & Co, Sydney, Australia (packet weighing 75 g)

Add up the total of all stamps used. Deduct this from the £12 with which you started. The amount left will be carried over to the next day.

▶ *What is a franking machine?*

This machine prints on an envelope, postcard or sticky label (used for parcels) in coloured ink the value of a stamp, as well as the date, time, place of posting, Post Office licence number and an advertising slogan if required. It saves time when preparing mail, makes a record of all postage used and is easier to keep secure than stamps.

Franking machines can be bought or hired from manufacturers such as Pitney Bowes and Roneo, but a Post Office licence is also required. There are two meters on the machine – one that shows how many postage units have been used to date (ascending register), the other which shows how many postage units are left in the machine (descending register). When the descending register is low, this means that more postage units need to be bought from the Post Office.

It is important not to let the descending register run too low, because this may result in postage units running out and mail missing the Post Office deadline. Some machines allow a small part to be lifted off which can be taken to the local Post Office, who use a special key to open the machine and add units, once payment has been made.

Modern, computerised franking machines are often linked to a Post Office computer and can have credits added simply by making a telephone call. The Post Office computer will automatically print an invoice and send it to the user of the franking machine. Modern machines can use a credit card system which allows credits to be added to the machine by simply inserting a plastic card.

Fig 6.15 Franking mark

Fig 6.16 An electronic franking machine

Franking machines can be locked to prevent dishonest use. The machine has to be set with the day's date each morning before use and the ink roller must be regularly re-inked. If a franking is incorrect, the envelope should be put to one side and used, if possible, later in the day. Otherwise, the franked item can be taken to the Post Office, which will give a refund, less 5 per cent. If a franking machine is taken to the Post Office for credits to be added, a record card is completed showing units used and units purchased.

When franking mail, the counter on the machine can be set to the amount of postage required, so that all items can be put through quickly and easily, without the need to find the correct value if using postage stamps. Franked mail can pass through the Post Office much faster as the franking on each item does not require cancelling in the same way as postage stamps. However, franked mail does have to be posted in a special way – either handed in over the counter of a post office, tied in separate first-class and second-class bundles facing the same way, or posted in a letter-box in a special envelope marked 'franked mail'. Some organisations provide red Post Office bags for first-class mail and green bags for second-class mail, and special mail items are placed in a yellow bag.

▶ *What about security?*

Firstly, remember that stamps are worth money and should be locked away until needed. Petty cash is normally used to buy stamps and should also be kept locked in a special tin box out of sight to prevent temptation. Incoming remittances in the form of cheques, postal orders, cash or stamps are also valuable, so make sure that you enter each remittance received into the Remittances Book and get the book signed – remember that this acts as your receipt and, if one remittance should go missing, it cannot be blamed on you.

The franking machine should also be kept locked and out of the way until it is required. It should only be used for business and not personal use. If a mistake is made, never throw the envelope or label away, but try to use it later or get a refund from the Post Office. Do not be afraid to admit that you have made a mistake. Your supervisor would prefer to get a refund, less 5 per cent, than find out you have been throwing your mistakes in the bin!

■ DIY 6.2.7

Below, you will find paragraphs that are incomplete. They are relevant to work already covered. Copy out these paragraphs and fill in the missing word(s), which you can select from the following lists.

1 *parcels ascending value descending*
2 *date locked ink licence*
3 *five counter postage quicker refund*
4 *letter first handed franked second*

1 A franking machine prints the _ _ _ _ _ of a stamp on an envelope, postcard or sticky label (used for _ _ _ _ _ _ _ _). There are two meters on the machine – one that shows how many units have been used to date, which is called the _ _ _ _ _ _ _ _ _ _ register, and one that shows how many units are left in credit, which is called the _ _ _ _ _ _ _ _ _ _ _ register.

2 You need a Post Office _ _ _ _ _ _ _ _ to operate a franking machine. Franking machines can be _ _ _ _ _ _ to prevent dishonest use. The machine is set with the day's _ _ _ _ and the _ _ _ roller regularly re-inked.

3 Franked mail can pass through the Post Office much _ _ _ _ _ _ _ than ordinary mail with postage stamps; there is also no need for different values of stamps to be kept as the machine has a _ _ _ _ _ _ _ that can be set with the exact _ _ _ _ _ _ _ required. If an incorrect franking is made, this can be taken to the post office for a _ _ _ _ _ _, although they will deduct _ _ _ _ per cent of the value.

4 Franked mail has to be either _ _ _ _ _ _ over the post office counter, tied in separate bundles for _ _ _ _ _class and _ _ _ _ _ _ class, or posted in a _ _ _ _ _ _ box in a special envelope marked '_ _ _ _ _ _ _' mail.

Completing Element 6.2

To complete this element on preparing for despatch outgoing/internal mail, you will need to put all DIY tasks in your folder and carry out a final assessment. This assessment must include the routine and urgent despatch of all categories of outgoing mail using standard Post Office guides and procedures. Competence must be demonstrated by dealing with a minimum of 10 consecutive items on a minimum of three separate occasions. The use of Post Office services or express delivery services and agencies is acceptable. If you are responsible for outgoing mail at work, you will be able to get credit for this by showing your tutor or assessor what you do. For this, complete a log over a period of time detailing all your outgoing mail activities.

Claiming credit

Once you have completed your final assessment, you will need to write in your record book or folder *how, when, where* and *what* you have done to prove that you are competent.

The following is an example of how one trainee completed this claim:

6.2.a While in the college training office, I checked the supervisor's outgoing letters for signature and enclosures. I reported omissions immediately.

6.2.b I used DL sized envelopes for the paperwork and padded bags for larger items. Parcels were wrapped according to the Post Office's *Wrap up Well* leaflet.

6.2.c All mail was addressed according to Post Office requirements.

6.2.d Scales were used to weigh heavy items and the *Postal Rates* leaflet used to calculate postage.

6.2.e Franked mail was placed in green or red bags ready for collection at 3.00 pm. Registered or recorded items were taken to the post office.

6.2.f The training office franking control card was completed each day. While on work experience at Coopers & Co I completed a postage book each day.

6.2.g At Coopers & Co I kept the stamps locked in the petty cash tin in a secure drawer. At college the franking machine was locked when not in use and kept in a locked cabinet.

UNIT 7
Reprographics

■ Element 7.1
PRODUCE COPIES FROM ORIGINAL DOCUMENTS USING REPROGRAPHIC EQUIPMENT

▶ *What does reprographic mean?*

Reproducing (making more) graphics (documents, drawings, graphs, etc) means, put simply, making more copies of an original. There are many different ways of making a copy of a document. 'Copying' usually refers to photocopying, and 'duplicating' refers to making copies from a master or stencil, which needs to be specially prepared.

The most common form of copying in an office used to be carbon paper copies. Carbon paper is ink-coated paper which is placed between two sheets of paper, so that typing or writing on the top sheet of paper produces a carbon copy on the second piece of paper. Although some offices still rely on this method of making copies, most now have a photocopier or may instruct their computer to produce a second copy.

▶ *What methods might you be expected to use?*

It will depend on the type of office in which you work and how many copies you need to make. The method chosen must take into account:

1 How many copies are needed?
2 How many pages are in the document?
3 How quickly is it needed?
4 What quality is required?

Carbon paper has a dull side and a glossy side. It is the glossy side that makes the copy.

The glossy side of the carbon is put against the paper on which the copy is to be made.

When papers are assembled for making carbon copies there is always one sheet of typing paper more than of carbon paper

Fig 7.1 Inserting carbon paper for carbon copies

Offset Litho

If your organisation needs to make a large quantity of copies, which are of a reasonable quality, it may be worth buying an offset litho machine.

This machine will need a specially trained operator, and the company providing the machine usually arranges for training. The offset litho can produce between 500–50,000 copies from one master, called a plate. A plate may be made from paper, plastic or metal. Paper plates are most usual as they are the cheapest, and they can produce between 500–1000 or more copies before they start to break. The plate can be prepared by typing or handwriting, but most are photocopied from the original documents. Plates can also be prepared by using special equipment, such as a plate-maker, or they can be professionally prepared by a printer. It is unlikely that you will need to know how to use an offset litho, but you may need to know about the process when recommending to your manager what type of system to use for copying. The copies made from an offset litho are excellent quality, and it is a suitable process for all business stationery, such as letterheaded paper and compliment slips, as well as form letters and circulars, minutes of meetings and staff handbooks, etc.

■ DIY 7.1.1

Test your knowledge so far – write out the following sentences, filling in the

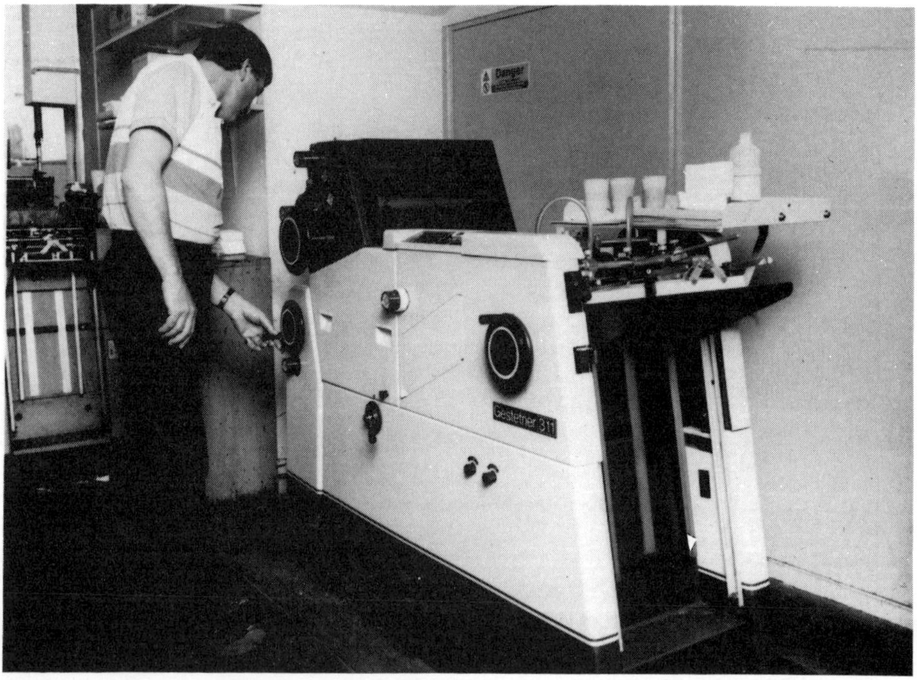

Fig 7.2 Offset litho printer

missing words from the ones provided below.

1 Reprographics means making _ _ _ _ _ _ of documents.

2 Offset litho machines can make between _ _ _ and _ _ _ _ _ copies from one master.

3 The master for an offset litho machine is called a _ _ _ _ _.

4 A plate may be made from _ _ _ _ _ or _ _ _ _ _ _ _ _ or _ _ _ _ _.

5 Offset litho copies can be used for all business _ _ _ _ _ _ _ _ _ _.

Words: plate paper stationery copies plastic 500 metal 50,000

Ink duplicators

These machines are still fairly common and are used by secretaries and general clerical staff. The masters prepared for these machines are called stencils. The stencil sheet is wax, which needs to be cut to allow ink to pass through on to the paper. Stencils can be prepared on the typewriter, where the keys cut the wax; or a scanner can be used which has a stylus to cut the wax; or a stylus pen can be used for

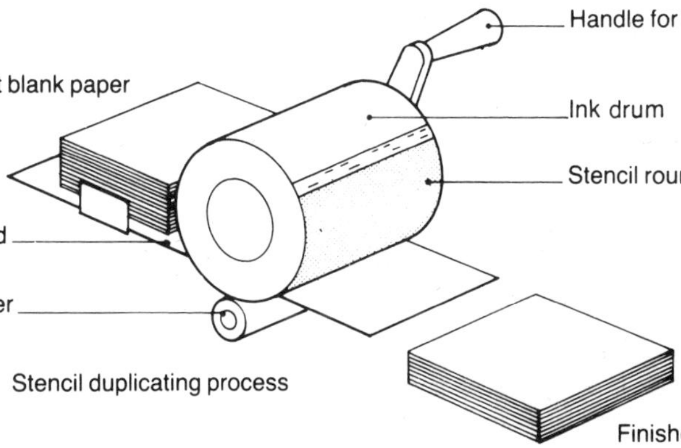

Fig 7.3 Ink duplicating process

handwriting. It is also possible to use heat to burn the wax, but a special wax stencil needs to be used for this. If you use a word processor that has an impact printer (see page 76) you will probably be able to make stencils on this as well.

An ink duplicating machine has a large drum covered in felt, and the stencil has a piece of card at the top with shaped holes cut out, which fit over a section on the drum. The stencil wraps around the drum and is held in place by a holding bar at the bottom. The ink is placed inside the drum and it oozes through the holes in the stencil on to the paper which passes under the turning drum once the machine is started up. The paper has to be partly absorbent (a bit like blotting paper) to allow the ink to soak into it and dry quickly. Although machines are now available which use ordinary paper and quick-drying ink. Different ink colours can be used inside the drum and an organisation that uses this type of duplicating will usually keep a different drum for each colour. It is very messy to clean all the ink out of a drum and to get the felt spotlessly clean. A different stencil will be needed for each different ink. For example, if you wanted three paragraphs on a page, with the first paragraph in black ink, the second in red and the third in black again, two stencils would be needed. The first stencil would have the first and last paragraphs on it (with a gap in the middle to allow for the second paragraph). All the copies needed would be duplicated with the black ink, and then be allowed to dry. The black ink drum would be taken off the ink duplicator and the red drum inserted. The second stencil would be put on the drum and the copies made would be passed a second time through the machine, this time with the second paragraph being printed in red ink in the gap left.

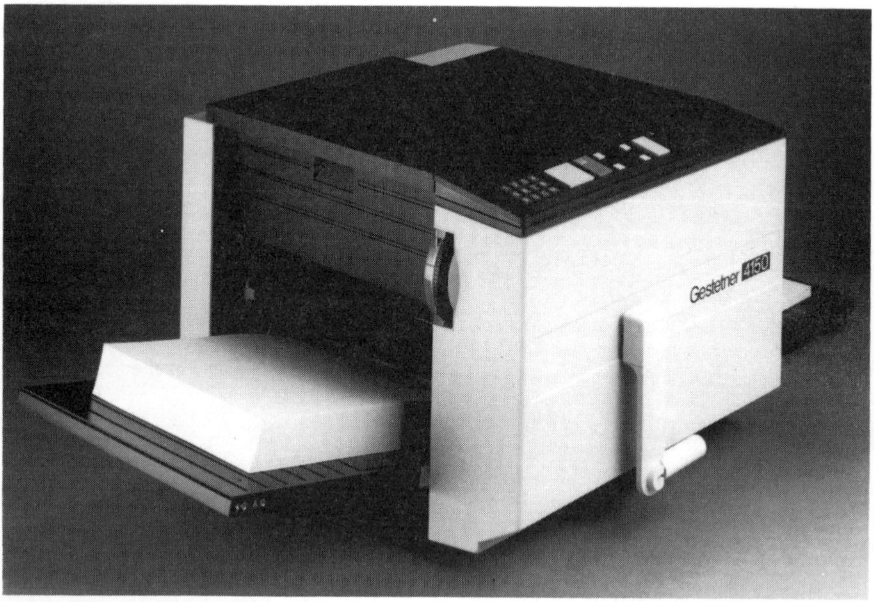

Fig 7.4 Ink duplicator

Although a duplicating machine does not require specialist training, it can be messy if used by an inexperienced operator. Without sufficient knowledge, changing inks or drums and removing a stencil can be awkward. Many companies supplying ink duplicating machines will include training for staff when the machine is bought. The copies made on ink duplicators are of a reasonable quality and suitable for internal use, eg for staff notices, memos or instructions. A stencil will usually produce up to 500 copies easily and some have been known to produce 5000. However, after 1000 copies, the ink usually starts to soak the stencil, sticking to the paper, and the stencil starts to tear. This will result in the ink seeping through on to the copies and producing a mess!

■ DIY 7.1.2

Answer the following questions, writing your answers in full to show you understand the process.

1 How many copies can an ink duplicator make?
2 What is the master for an ink duplicator called?
3 Can a word processor be used to make a master?
4 Do I need to train staff especially to use an ink duplicator?

5 How many copies could I reasonably make from a stencil?
6 Can colour copies be made?
7 Can I use this method of reproduction to send letters to my customers?

Computers and word processors

If you are using a computer or WP with an impact printer, you may be able to use carbon paper to take extra copies of your documents – this would be very economical. However, carbon copies are not very good quality and, although they are suitable for file copies, they are not good enough for external use. Many clerk typists will make an extra copy, using their printer instead of using a photocopier. Whether or not this is costing the organisation more, will depend on the type of printer used and the type of photocopier available. Some of the larger, complicated photocopiers are only worth using if you are making at least six copies of a document.

Photocopiers

The most common machine used in offices for reprographics is the photocopier. The facilities available on machines vary a great deal: small machines have very few facilities, and some of the large machines do everything but make the tea! The majority of copiers do not need special paper. The document to be copied is placed on a glass top, which is covered by a rubber and plastic lid, or it may be fed into the machine. If more than 200 copies of a document are required, it may be worth considering ink or offset duplicating.

▶ *What basic facilities would you be expected to use?*

The basic photocopiers available will carry out the following functions:

- copying 1–99 copies of an A4 sheet
- reducing A4 to A5
- enlarging A5 to A4

More advanced copiers (sometimes called smart copiers) will also:

- copy using larger and smaller sizes of paper
- copy using both sides of the paper (back-to-back copying, called duplexing)
- arrange the copies in page number order (collate)
- accept card and plastic transparencies

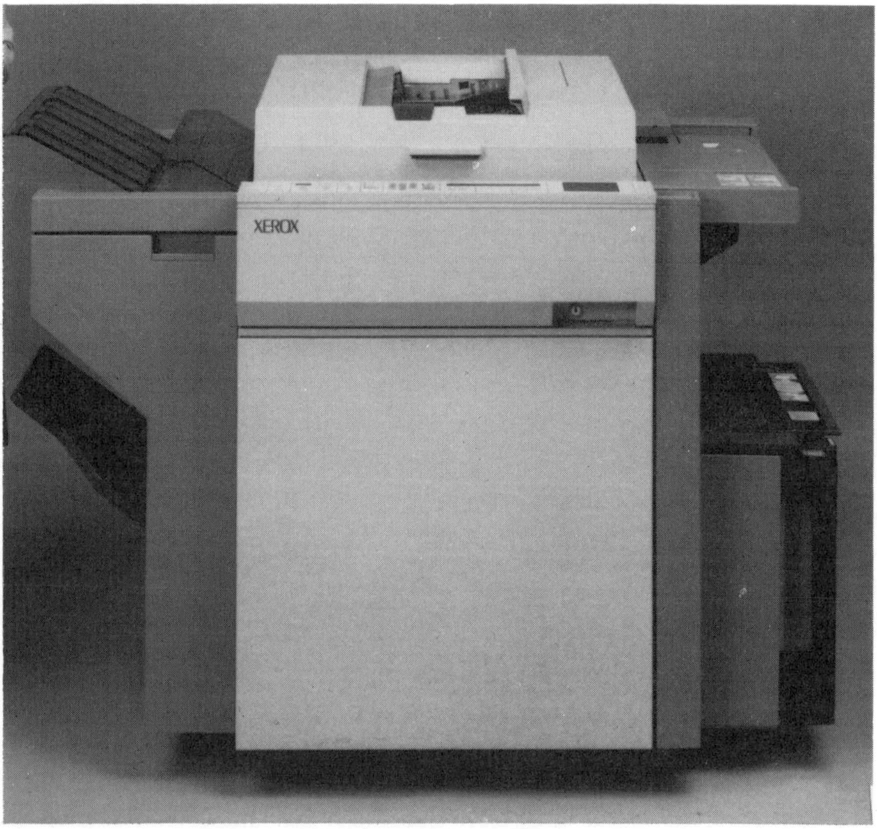

Fig 7.5 A photocopier

- automatically feed in the pages to be copied (automatic document feeder (ADF))
- staple the sheets together when the copying has finished
- make colour copies (these machines are expensive and not common in general offices)

What is collating?

This means putting the documents in the correct page order. Pages will usually be numbered using arabic numbers eg 1, 2, 3, or small roman numerals, eg i, ii, iii. You should be familiar with both. If you have 25 copies of a 30-page report to make, it will take some time to put the pages in the correct order. You will need to have a work area where the 30 pages can be placed in separate heaps. Alternatively, you will have to sort the first 10 pages (or however many you can lay out) followed by the second set of 10 pages and then the third. These three heaps would then have to be collated into the final sets. You will need to lay out the documents in a logical sequence, either in page number order or, to speed up the process, an order where both hands can work at the same time. For example, a 10-page document could be laid out as follows:

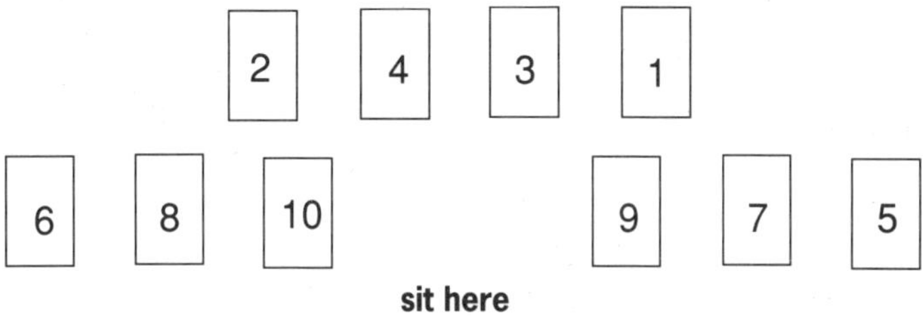

The left hand will take one copy of page 10 and place it in the space in front, and then the right hand will take one copy of page 9 and place it on top of page 10. Both hands can move at the same time and the document is collated back to front. Complete sets can be stacked away from the work area.

Collator. If you are lucky, your organisation may have a machine to do this job for you, called a collator. If you are asked to carry out a lot of collating, it may be worth investigating the cost of a collating machine. Machines are also available to automatically collate, staple and fold documents.

Jogger. Another machine which helps in a print room is a jogger. The photocopied documents are placed in the jogger and it shakes them together so that the corners are neatly together before the document is stapled.

Stapling may be an automatic process in some photocopiers. If you do the stapling, you may use a manual stapler or an electric one – take care with an electric ones as it is fast and likely to make you jump when you use it, so keep your fingers out of the way!

Duplexing (back-to-back copying) can be carried out on a basic machine by feeding the same sheet of paper into the machine again. This reduces the amount of paper used, so is cost effective. It also reduces the amount of paper that has to be circulated, which may reduce postal costs (if the document is to be posted to customers, for example), or reduce the amount of space required for filing (if the document is being distributed to staff).

Computers. The most intelligent photocopiers combine computing with copying. Information can be entered on to a computer and stored, and this can then be recalled and automatically printed directly by the copier without having a 'hard' copy (original copy) to print from. It is also possible to network a photocopying machine to allow it to receive and send information to and from distant computers.

■ DIY 7.1.3

You have been asked to look after Sara, a trainee from school on work experience. Sara asks you to explain the following words that she has heard the staff use when referring to photocopying. From what you have read above (and using a dictionary if you wish), write out your explanation so that Sara can understand the meanings of the terms.

1 Reprographics
2 Collate
3 Reduced copies
4 Enlarged copies
5 Stapling
6 Duplexing
7 ADF
8 Cost effective
9 Networked machines
10 Jogger

Sometimes you may be asked to include a picture or diagram in the middle of a document. If the diagram cannot be typed or word processed, the typist will leave a space big enough for the diagram to be inserted. Usually this is done by gluing the diagram or picture in place, and your original may look messy, but the copies should look perfect. This process is called 'cutting and pasting'. In the same way, there may be a part of the document that your manager does not want copied and it is possible to put a plain piece of paper over the paragraph or drawing that is not required and photocopy the remainder. This process is called 'masking'.

Whichever type of copier you use, make sure you are familiar with the recommended user instructions. If you are unsure on how to operate a machine, read the manufacturer's manual or ask someone who is familiar with the machine.

▶ *What health and safety points should you remember?*

Any machine using electricity should be away from the wall to allow the air to circulate around it. This helps to cool the machine when it is being used. The electric cable should not trail across a floor where people are walking, eg across a doorway or gangway. It should be switched off at night and the plug taken out. *Never* put any fluids near a copier – not even correcting fluid. Do not be tempted to put your hands inside the machine, unless you know exactly what you are doing. The machine should be regularly maintained, by an expert. This can usually be arranged through the supplier, or if you rent your machine, it is likely to be part of the agreement.

▶ *What will you be able to repair on the machine?*

The type of problem that regularly causes a machine to stop is paper running out or jamming somewhere inside the machine. However, you should not attempt to correct these problems unless you have been shown how to do this by someone who knows. When replacing the paper there is usually a paper tray that needs to be filled. The paper should be taken out of the protective wrapping paper carefully and used the right way up. The label on the protective cover is usually the right way up, or if you pass your finger and thumb carefully along the edge of a piece of paper you can usually feel which is the 'sharper' side. When the paper is cut at the factory, the edge of the paper is very slightly bent down. The paper should be placed in the machine the same way as it was cut – this will help to reduce paper jams. Most machines have a special sign that flashes when the paper has run out.

A machine jam may easily be put right. If you open the front of a photocopier, there is normally a set of coloured handles or numbered parts. These will indicate where a jam is likely to occur If you can see the paper, then the position of the jam is likely to be obvious. Otherwise you may have to work through the positions one at a time. Be careful when you remove the paper not to tear it because, if a little piece is left inside, it will probably be enough to jam the next sheet.

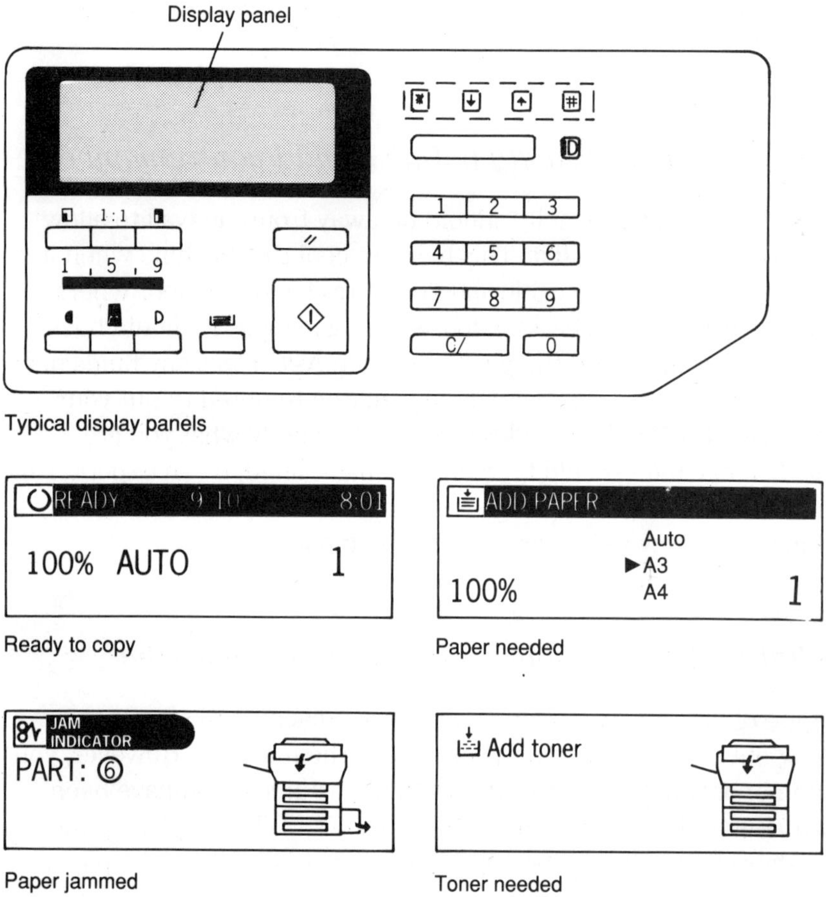

Fig 7.6 Diagram showing the indicating panel on a typical photocopier

Another common cause of the machine stopping, or not producing copies, is when it runs out of toner. This is the powder ink that the machine uses to create the image. The toner is attracted to the drum of the machine like a magnet. The drum rolls the image on to the paper and the paper is quickly heated to get the toner to set. Sometimes when you are unjamming a piece of paper you will find that the toner on the paper is still dry and rubs off on your hands. This is because it has not yet passed through the heat process. Before the toner runs out completely, the quality of the copies obtained from the machine is likely to become poor. You will probably know that the toner is low and will need replacing soon, but a light on the copier will flash to indicate that toner is low or out.

Toner is supplied in cartridges and new ones should not under any circumstances be opened. When removing the old cartridge, make sure that you do not spill any toner on your hands or clothes. If it does get on your hands, wash them in cold water. When the new cartridge is placed into the machine, a strip of paper or foil is pulled back allowing the toner to drop into the machine.

Sometimes, when a document has been corrected with fluid, it has not been given enough time to dry before someone has taken a photocopy. The result is a mark on the glass of the machine and a copy with a blotch on it, where the fluid has spread. Any marks such as this should be removed from the glass with a damp cloth (not a wet cloth), but stubborn marks may need a little spirit, such as thinners, on them. Keep away from the glass anything that may scratch or mark it, otherwise all future photocopies will have a similar mark on them.

■ DIY 7.1.4

List all the facilities of a photocopier to which you have access. Check whether the indicating lights are the same as those above and, if not, draw them and write the meanings by the side. Find out where the supplies of paper and toner are kept, and who is responsible for reordering and when these orders are sent. Write your findings in a memo to John, a new member of staff who has joined the Sales Department of your company.

▶ *What if the machine fault cannot be repaired?*

The maintenance engineer should be called to correct any fault which cannot easily be put right. Most engineers will call within 24 hours as they appreciate the urgency of the matter. Make sure that you tell your colleagues and supervisors that the machine is out of action and that there will be a delay in getting the copying finished. This is extremely important, especially if your colleagues have a deadline to meet and need the copies urgently.

▶ *How is a multi-page document held together?*

There are many different methods of securing documents apart from stapling them. Some need special equipment but others are cheap and as efficient as stapling.

Paperclips

Paperclips come in different sizes, from quite small to huge (up to 50mm–75mm long). They are quick and easy to use and fairly cheap to buy. The disadvantage with them is that they tend to pick up other documents when they are kept in a pile.

Treasury tags

To use tags, holes need to be punched in the document, either in the top left-hand corner or half-way down the left-hand side. The treasury tags have plastic strips at each end and one is threaded through the hole. Tags are available in different colours and lengths, with longer ones for the bulky documents. They are quick, cheap and efficient to use, but are not really suitable for sending documents externally.

Ring binders

Once again, the document would have to be hole punched. Ring binders may have two or four rings and come in different sizes. They are quite expensive and would not be the normal way of securing everyday documents. However, they are extremely useful for items such as staff handbooks or a set of instructions.

Spiral binding

This process needs a special machine which is used to punch oblong holes along the edge of the document, and to open up the teeth of the plastic spiral. The pages are fed carefully on to the open teeth, and when the last page has been positioned the teeth can be closed, securing the document. Metal continuous spirals are also used in this way, except that the spiral is pushed on from the bottom to the top of the document. Electric machines are available that will carry out the whole process and would be a useful piece of equipment to any office that regularly produces booklets requiring binding. The result is a professional look to the document which is suitable for internal and external use.

Flat comb binder

This is a similar process to the spiral binding, the difference being that two plastic strips are used, one with spikes and one with holes. Holes are punched in the document and the spikes are pushed through the holes. The holed strip is then pushed over the spikes and is heat

Fig 7.7 A plastic comb binder

sealed, the document being secured between the two plastic strips. Again a professional look is obtained but special equipment is required that is quite expensive to purchase.

Slide binder

A slide binder is the easiest to use, and is quite cheap, but is not so useful. The binder is made from solid plastic and is slid along the edge of the document (no hole punching is needed). The pages are held firmly but they can be difficult to keep open when reading, as the book will not stay open flat on a desk. Although this is not essential, a plastic tray with guidelines is available, which helps to get the binder on easily and in the correct place.

Heat binding

This gives the document a professional look, similar to a paperback book. The document has a gummed strip placed along the edge and this is put into a heat machine which locks the strip into place. Once cool, the document can be handled without fear of losing the pages. Special equipment is required and this is expensive, so it would not be worth buying unless a lot of binding is required.

If you meet any problems in collating and securing your documents, make sure that you inform your supervisor. You should also tell your colleagues of the delay that will occur in getting the finished work back to them.

► *How can you make sure that material waste is kept to a minimum?*

The material used most when copying is paper. To make sure that waste is reduced, follow these simple guidelines.

1 Place the document to be copied carefully on to the clean glass of the photocopier and make sure it is the right way round. (Use the guide arrows on the machine.)

2 If you need a lot of copies, try making one first to ensure it is all right. Alter the density (lighten or darken the copy) if necessary. When you have a good copy, the remaining copies can be made.

3 If you are copying back-to-back, always try one first, to make sure that the second side is the right way up.

4 Keep a tray for any wasted 'first tries'. These can be used on the other side, or can be cut up for use as rough paper in the office.

5 Use the back-to-back facility whenever possible, as this reduces by half the amount of paper required.

6 Reduce copies whenever possible, such as A3 to A4, but make sure the final document is still easy to read!

7 Do not make extra copies 'just in case'. Only copy the amount required.

8 Do not store the paper anywhere damp, as damp paper will jam in the machine.

9 Restrict staff use to essential work and do not allow personal work to be carried out.

10 Make sure that the document to be copied is suitable for copying. For instance, some coloured papers will not copy, eg dark orange, and photographs do not always copy well; some other documents may be too light to give clear copies.

11 If you have been interrupted while copying, make sure that you are at the correct place before starting again. Quite often people will ask to 'jump the queue' for just one copy, but this can be quite off-putting if you are in the middle of a long and complicated job.

■ DIY 7.1.5

The costs of reprographics can be one of the most expensive items for a business, taking into account the paper, toner, rent for the machine, maintenance and electricity. Most businesses will try to calculate how much each copy costs so that this cost can be charged to the customers or clients for whom they are doing the work. Calculate how much each copy cost in one week when the payments made for materials, etc, were:

Paper 10 reams (500 sheets in each ream) at £3 per ream	=
Toner 1 cartridge at £30	=
Rent and maintenance for 1 week £40	=
Electricity (estimated) for 1 week £2	=

Total the costs and divide by 5,000 (the number of sheets used)

= the number of pence per copy.

Compare this cost with the cost per copy of the machine you use.

▶ *How can staff use of copiers be supervised?*

Some organisations use a record book to record how many copies are made by each member of staff and each department. This book may be kept by the photocopier operator, if there is one, or it may be filled in by each person using the machine. If it is left to each individual to fill in, the copier counter needs to be checked regularly to make sure that people are being honest. If the counter number and the book record are totally different, another method of recording may need to be found. This could mean employing a photocopier operator who will carry out all requests and keep a log of work carried out.

Some machines may have a special card reader supplied as an accessory. Each member of staff is issued with a 'credit' card that will allow them to make copies, up to the maximum credited on the card. The card is slid across the reader and the copier will then allow the user to make copies. The card works in a similar way to a telephone card, in that each time the card is used the units are reduced on the card. Once the maximum has been reached, the machine will not allow any more copies to be made. The card will have to be returned to the main office for renewal.

Another system in use, which is similar to the credit card is a copier which has a keyboard attached to it. Each member of staff is given a PIN number (Personal Identity Number). This number must be keyed in before the machine will operate. Each PIN number will have a maximum number of copies allowed, this information being stored in the memory of the keyboard. Once this number is reached the machine will not allow any more copies to be made.

Larger organisations may invest in a central reprographic section, which may have a smart copier, and this section will carry out all requests for large numbers of copies (for example anything more than five copies). The costs can be reduced but the time taken to send the document to the repro section and get it returned may be a disadvantage.

■ DIY 7.1.6

Design a form that can be filled in by staff when using the copier. It should include the date, name of staff member, department, number of copies made and the copier counter number. Type or word process your example and use it to record the copies you make over the next month. This record will be an essential part of your evidence.

► *Can any documents be copied?*

The copying of documents is controlled by the Copyright, Designs and Patents Act 1988. It is illegal to copy documents that are protected and the symbol © is printed, normally on the first page or the back of the first page of the document, or inside the front cover. If you look at the front pages of this book you will find the symbol as well as a statement that copying is not allowed. However, some documents may be copied if it is for educational purposes and others may be copied if the author's permission is obtained first. You should always check before copying that the document you wish to copy is not protected. Obviously if the document has been written by someone in the office it will be all right to copy it. The Act also covers copyright in music and video tapes, records, TV and radio programmes, and computer programs.

▪ DIY 7.1.7

Visit your local library and read a summary of the Copyright Act. Most libraries have on display an excerpt from the Act or will be able to find a reference for you.

Jenny is always asking you to copy articles from magazines and books. In your own words write a memo to Jenny, telling her what restrictions there are on copying other people's published work.

Completing Unit 7

To complete this element on reprographics you will need to put all the DIY tasks in your work folder, and carry out a final assessment. This assessment must cover copying from A5, A4 and A3 documents, and using enlarging and reducing facilities on documents of more than one page. Any type of reprographic equipment may be used and collating may be carried out by machine or hand. You should keep a record of work carried out that covers a minimum of one month and get the record signed by your supervisor. You should be prepared to answer questions about the type of faults that may occur with a machine and how to correct them; how to keep material waste to a minimum; and what reprographic recording procedures you are aware of.

Claiming credit

Once you have completed your final assessment, you will need to write in your record book or folder *how, when, where* and *what* you have done to prove you are competent.

The following is an example of how one trainee completed this claim.

7.1.a During my work experience for 2 weeks at Coopers & Co, I carried out photocopying on A4 and A5 sheets. I always met the deadline set.

7.1.b I kept the material wastage to a minimum by backing up and reducing, and using waste for trial copies.

7.1.c All pages were put in the correct order. They were checked carefully.

7.1.d The documents were kept together by using staples, paperclips or tags.

7.1.e Originals and copies were delivered as requested by my colleagues and supervisors.

7.1.f When faults occurred, I corrected them where possible, as taught by my supervisor.

7.1.g If I could not complete the job, I told my colleague or supervisor immediately what the problem was.

7.1.h I completed the record book correctly, used the machine as instructed and made sure I followed all the safety procedures, eg no liquids near the machine.

UNIT 8
Liaising with callers and colleagues

Element 8.1
RECEIVE AND ASSIST CALLERS

Whether you work for a large or small organisation, the way in which you deal with callers is very important. A caller is anyone who comes to see you or your colleagues and does not work in your department on an everyday basis. This could be someone from:

- another department or section
- another branch
- another company or other organisation
- a customer or client
- people attending a meeting
- people delivering or collecting items
- people attending an interview or asking about vacancies

Some of these callers will be expected and others will be unexpected.

All of these people are classed as 'visitors' when they call on you for information or for your help. The way in which these visitors are greeted and your attitude to them is very important.

If you do not look presentable (neat and tidy clothes and hair), they may already be forming a poor impression of you before you even speak. If, when you speak, your language is poor or unclear they may not be convinced that you are able to help them and may doubt your ability, and this may lead to doubts about the organisation's products or services.

Businesses such as building societies and airlines have special uniforms for staff that deal with customers and clients. This makes sure that the staff are always neatly presented and do not wear clothes that may be considered 'unsuitable' for the office. It also gives the organisation an 'image' which the customers can associate with it – the staff are easily recognised. Staff do not have to buy suitable clothing to wear to work and have a feeling of 'belonging' to the organisation. Some organisations may also have rules about footwear, make-up and jewellery, for men and women.

■ DIY 8.1.1

1 Make a list of any item of clothing, footwear or jewellery that you believe to be unsuitable for wearing in an office where you deal with customers and callers.

2 Design a uniform that you would like to wear in an office, making sure that the colours are suitable and that the style is comfortable for all-day wear. You may like to select and cut out items from a catalogue or design your own. Present your designs in a suitable way to your tutor.

The way in which you greet your callers may depend on the organisation's policy and who the caller is. If they are staff from another department you may be familiar with them and use their first names. For example, you may say 'Hello John. What can I do for you?'. This is informal but polite and friendly. Normally the managers, directors and most senior members of staff would not be called by their first names.

External callers to the business are usually greeted by saying 'Good morning (or 'Good afternoon') How may I help you?' If you know their name, it is polite to use it: 'Good afternoon, Mrs James. How may I help you?' sounds more friendly and helpful. For regular external callers, such as representatives from other companies, delivery and post staff, cleaners, etc you will probably get to know their first names and greet them on an informal basis.

If you need to pass on an external caller to another member of staff, always find out the caller's name before explaining to your colleague how he/she can help. This will allow your colleague to use the person's name, which will leave the caller with a good impression.

▶ *What skills will you need?*

As soon as callers enter the room you should show that you have

Fig 8.1 A reception area

noticed them, by looking at them and smiling. If you are busy on the telephone, indicate that you will not be long. One of the most important skills is listening.

Listening. Very few people listen properly when someone is speaking to them. You should show callers that they have your full attention by looking at them and keeping eye contact, and stop doing whatever you were doing when they came in. Wait until the caller has finished speaking before you reply (even if you know the answer when callers are half-way through speaking, it is polite to let them finish). If you are unsure of what the caller wants, ask questions and, if you are still unsure, call your supervisor or a colleague to assist.

■ DIY 8.1.2

When receiving callers you should always try to be:

- polite
- courteous
- positive
- friendly

- helpful
- patient

and sometimes you will need to be:

- tactful
- diplomatic
- firm
- direct
- assertive

Make a list of these qualities and look them up in a dictionary if you are unsure of their meaning. Tick the ones you feel you are able to use now, when greeting callers, and put a cross by any quality you feel you need to work on. How can you improve the qualities that need working on?

Non-verbal signs. Not only will callers be getting an impression about you when they see you, but you will also have a first impression about them when they enter your office. Those callers who feel confident and know what they want will probably walk straight into the office and go up to a member of staff. Those callers who are unsure of what or who they want, may enter the office and hover by the door, looking round to see whether they can see anything or anyone familiar. Quite often these people are waiting for someone to approach them and offer help. You will need to try to *read the non-verbal signs of communication* (gestures, movements, facial expressions, eye contact): another skill to develop to help you deal with callers effectively. Reading body language can be very important when receiving callers, and it can assist you in identifying possible difficulties, such as aggressive visitors or suspicious callers.

DIY 8.1.3

Draw up a sheet with the two column headings shown below. Look at the next 10 people that walk into your room or go past you and try to think of a word that describes their body language.

Person	**Body language**	
1	confident	some examples:
2	shy	you may
3	angry	think of
4	unsure	others

Person	**Body language**
5	
6	
7	
8	
9	
10	

Speaking. Once you have listened to your caller, you will need to tell them how you can help and what will be done. Your *oral skills* are extremely important and are the most frequently-used method of communication. When you speak, use a friendly manner, speak reasonably slowly and in a clear voice. Always keep eye contact and speak directly to the caller. Avoid looking away from callers, even when giving directions, as they may not be able to hear what you say. If you need to interrupt a colleague, always apologise first 'Sorry to interrupt you but, …'. This helps to create a pleasant working atmosphere and relationship between staff members.

▶ *What else can you do to create a good impression?*

A clean and tidy reception area will always impress a caller, both in the main reception area and in your own office. Make sure that any deliveries are not placed in the way of callers and are moved as soon as possible. Callers who arrive irate, angry or anxious should be calmed down as quickly as possible. Listen to any complaints, but never agree that the complaint is justified; find someone who can deal with the problem as quickly as possible. If there is a delay, always keep the caller informed of what is going on. Offer tea/coffee to those callers that need to wait for a while or offer them an alternative appointment if they are unable to wait.

▶ *What if the caller asks for confidential information?*

Unless a caller is authorised, no confidential information should ever be given (verbal or written). Confidential information includes personal details of staff, their exact whereabouts and appointment schedule; financial details of the organisation and its customers; details of future projects or contracts, etc. If you are unsure whether information may be passed on or not, always check with your supervisor.

Many organisations now have strict rules about the security of the building. Visitors may not be allowed to walk round the offices without a member of staff with them. Usually a member of staff will collect the visitor from reception and accompany them to the meeting office. A receptionist should not leave reception unattended in case another caller arrives and is left to wander round the building unsupervised. In the majority of organisations visitors are still allowed to find their own way to the office they require. You must ensure that the directions given are clear and precise, otherwise the visitor may get lost.

When the visit has finished the member of staff with the visitor should make sure that he/she knows how to get out of the building. There may be a quicker exit door than the door by which they entered.

If you are escorting a visitor, make sure you keep to a steady pace. Make conversation about simple things such as the weather, if it is their first visit to the company, did they have problems finding the company, etc. Do not try to discuss their business with them. You may have to escort elderly or disabled visitors. Always walk at a pace that is comfortable for them and, if the visitor is blind, offer your arm and tell them when steps or corners are nearing. Foreign visitors or those with speech difficulties may find it hard to explain who or what they want. Have patience and do not finish off their sentences for them, or they may become anxious and flustered.

Some companies issue visitors with a badge or pass card to show that they have been approved to visit the building. Others may have a reception book to write down the details of all callers. In some cases, such as government offices, the caller may need to have their bag, briefcase or belongings searched before being allowed to enter the offices. In some extreme cases a body search may be carried out. Any organisation carrying out such procedures is likely to employ special staff such as security guards to attend to these duties.

■ DIY 8.1.4

Write down the directions for a person who wishes to get from the main reception, at your work or training centre, to your office or training room. Would these directions be clear to anyone? Could someone who is in a wheelchair manage unaided? What changes, if any, would you make for these people?

▶ *What information should you be able to access?*

Regardless of which office you are working in, you should always be able to put your hand on a copy of the internal telephone directory or telephone list and a copy of the organisation chart (the family tree of the company). This will tell you who works in which department, where they are located and perhaps their duties. It will help you to identify the person to whom you wish to refer a caller, if you are unable to help the caller yourself.

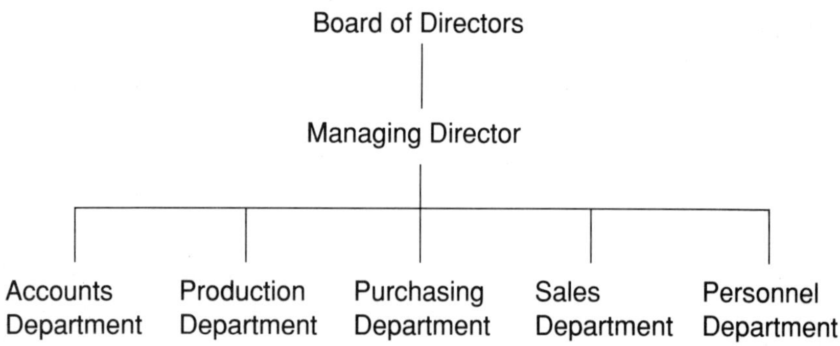

Fig 8.2 An organisation chart for a company

■ DIY 8.1.5

Draw an organisation chart of the company or other organisation where you work or where one of your friends or relations works. You do not need to put all the names of the staff (if you do not know them), but put the department names and a brief outline of the department's duties and responsibilities.

In addition you should be able to locate:

- local telephone directories
- local maps
- central services, such as bus station, railway station, taxi rank or telephone number

Telephone. You should also be familiar with your telephone system. You may need to obtain information from another department or obtain an external number to get information for your caller. This means you should know how to:

- obtain an internal number
- obtain an external number

- transfer an internal number (if possible)
- transfer an external number to another extension

You may need to get assistance quickly if you have an aggressive or suspicious caller, in which case you may need to dial an emergency number:

- be aware of any emergency number or security number within the company
- know how to dial the external emergency services

Completing Element 8.1

To complete this element on receiving and assisting callers you will need to put all the DIY tasks in your work folder and carry out a final assessment. This assessment should be a log book of *where, when, who* and *how* you dealt with at least 20 callers. For example you may draw up a log sheet as in Fig 8.3.

These callers may be people from your own organisation or external callers. In a training situation they may be colleagues, tutors or visitors to the training centre. The callers should include those who are expected and unexpected, routine and non-routine, internal and external to the organisation. It should also include at least two difficult and aggressive callers. You do not have to work on a main reception area to complete this element (that is covered in Unit 15 of Business Administration at Level 2).

Date	Name of caller	Reason for calling	Action taken

Fig 8.3 Log sheet

You should be prepared to answer questions on how to recognise and react to non-verbal communication (body language) and how to deal with aggressive and difficult callers. If you are currently working full-time or part-time, you may be able to claim some credit for the callers you already deal with. Discuss this with your tutor.

Claiming credit

Once you have completed your final assessment you will need to write in your record book or folder *how, when, where* and *what* you have done to prove that you are competent.

The following is how one trainee completed this claim.

8.1.a While I was on work experience for three weeks at Cold Service Ltd, I greeted callers from inside and outside the company (see log book in work folder). Callers to the company I greeted by saying 'Good morning. How may I help you?'; callers to my office I greeted by saying 'Hello. What can I do for you today?'.

8.1.b I made sure that I did not give any confidential information to any callers, internal or external, eg home telephone numbers of staff.

8.1.c I took visitors to the company to the correct office, and told callers from other departments who they needed and where to find them.

8.1.d If I could not help the caller immediately, or if the information needed was going to be delayed, I explained why it would be late and told the caller how long I estimated the wait would be. I made sure I kept the caller advised regularly of the situation.

8.1.e If the caller asked me things that I knew nothing about, I called my supervisor. If I was asked something about another department, I telephoned and asked a member of staff from that department to come and answer the questions or supply the goods needed.

■ Element 8.2

MAINTAIN BUSINESS RELATIONSHIPS WITH OTHER MEMBERS OF STAFF

We have already seen how important it is to deal with callers in a polite and courteous manner. Just as important is how you deal with colleagues – the people you work with.

A business will always have a better image if the staff are cheerful and content with their work. For staff to be happy they also need to be able to get on with each other. It is highly unlikely that all of the staff will like each other all of the time, as arguments and upsets will happen sometimes. However, if everybody tries to get along with each other, the number of arguments occurring should be reduced. It is also important to settle any difficulties as quickly as possible and let normal routine return.

When selecting new staff, the managers will try to appoint someone who can do the job but who will also 'fit in' with the existing staff. This is because they want a team of staff who will be willing to assist each other and work together for the good of the business. It is not always possible to decide at interview whether a person has exactly the right type of personality, qualities and skills to fit into the existing staff team, but with experience a good manager will identify whether a person is likely to have most of the necessary qualities.

When a person is first appointed to a new section or department, it is up to the existing staff to make sure that their new colleague settles in as quickly as possible. The first few days can be quite uncomfortable for new members of staff if the rest of the staff do not make them feel welcome. They will not work to the best of their ability and will be unlikely to want to stay.

■ DIY 8.2.1

Make a list of all the things which you could do for a newly appointed clerk in your office. Assume you have been working at the company for the last year and are familiar with all the procedures.

▶ *How can you make a team work more effectively?*

A good team is one that can work together well when members are very busy or when there are quiet periods. During the busy times you will probably have plenty to keep you occupied, but it is important that you still assist your colleagues when they need help. It could be that they have an important deadline to meet for the manager and need assistance with some of the more routine tasks. At this time you need to be able to sort out your own work into a priority order, so that the most important work gets completed first. The work that is not so urgent may be left for a day or so. You may find that, when a very urgent job comes into the office, everyone is working on it at the same time, to meet the deadline. This could mean working through the normal lunch break and later than the normal finishing time.

When your colleagues ask you to assist it is important to show that you are willing to help whenever you can. In this way a team spirit is developed and the working atmosphere is good.

You should also make sure that you are reliable and honest. If you tell a colleague that you will do something, make sure you do it. Your colleague will rely on you to keep your word and, if you don't, you will be letting your team down. You should also do the job to the best of your ability, not hurry it to such an extent that you make mistakes. The job will only have to be done again, by someone responsible. Do not get yourself a reputation for being unreliable.

Find out what your colleagues' responsibilities are. You should be totally familiar with their work area, so that if additional work comes into the department, you know who is likely to be responsible for it. Some departments, such as sales and purchasing, may be responsible for customers according to their name, ie alphabetically. For example, one member of staff would deal with customers whose name begins with A–F, another with G–P and a third with Q–Z. If the first person becomes extremely busy, one of the others should be prepared to help out for a while, or if the situation continues perhaps some of the customers need to be reallocated.

■ DIY 8.2.2

You work in an office with two others. You get on really well with one of them, but not with the other. Both of them need your help in getting some photocopying completed for an important client. Your friend has almost finished, but you would prefer to help your friend rather than your other colleague.

1 Which of the two would you help?
2 What would you say to the one you are not going to help?

When you receive instructions from colleagues, make sure you understand them fully before completing the job. The instructions may be given to you verbally or in writing. If verbal, repeat to your colleague what is wanted, just to check you have understood correctly. Write down a list of the jobs you have been given, if there is more than one. If jobs are written down for you, read through these instructions carefully and check any words that you cannot read or understand. Always check if you are unsure, as you may waste time and materials doing the job incorrectly.

▶ *What if you are unable to help when asked?*

Quite often you may find that you have too much work to finish yourself to be able to stop and give your colleagues a hand. All you need to do is explain to them what you are doing and how important it is.

If a colleague disagrees with you and feels that his or her work is more important, discuss it between you. If both of you are unable to agree, then you will need to see the supervisor or manager and let them decide which work has priority. It is always best for colleagues to settle disagreements between them if possible, otherwise an unfriendly working atmosphere may occur. It is sometimes difficult to tell a superior such as your manager, that you are too busy to help. Once again, you should explain why you cannot help. If the decision is made that your work can wait, you should carry out the superior's work willingly.

Do not be frightened to tell your colleagues or manager when you are not getting work completed to the deadlines. It could be that you have far too much to do and need help.

▶ *What difficulties might you face in working relationships?*

You may find that you work with someone whom you dislike or who dislikes you – a personality clash. This difficulty should not be allowed to interfere with the work carried out in the office. Try to be polite and courteous at all times and do not gossip to others about the person. If you hear rumours about someone in the office, do not repeat them. Gossip can cause many problems – whether it is true or not.

Quite often problems that cause difficulties in working relationships are personal problems. For example, body odour; too strong a perfume or cologne; unsuitable clothes or unclean clothes/hair/nails; habits such as smoking, sniffing, eating strong-smelling foods and talking whilst eating; chewing gum; biting nails; jangling jewellery; etc.

■ DIY 8.2.3

List the things that would most annoy you, if someone constantly did them in an office. Which of these things could you put up with, and which would you have to do something about? What would you do?

Things likely to annoy me	I could put up with	I could not put up with	Action I would take

Other problems may occur if a personal relationship develops between two people in the same office. There is nothing wrong with going out with someone from the same office, as long as the relationship develops outside the office and not during work time. It is difficult for other staff to work with colleagues who are constantly discussing their social plans, disappearing to be with each other, or making suggestive comments to each other.

Perhaps more difficult to cope with is someone who is constantly trying to 'chat-up' other members of staff. Quite often the attention received by this person is not wanted and can become a real nuisance. Tell the person concerned in a firm but polite manner, that you are not interested, and do not do anything to encourage the comments. Do not embarrass the person in front of other colleagues as this may be humiliating and could lead to an attempt to do the same to you later. If the situation becomes too difficult to cope with, discuss it with your supervisor. If the person concerned is your supervisor, then you should discuss it with the personnel officer or someone who is responsible and in whom you can confide. If the situation develops into a serious problem, then you may wish to see a solicitor or advice bureau who can advise you on sexual harassment matters.

Completing Element 8.2

To complete this element on maintaining business relationships with other members of staff, you will need to put all DIY tasks in your work folder and carry out a final assessment. This assessment must include an observation of your response to colleagues' requests and working with others. You should be prepared to answer questions on possible difficulties that may arise with office relationships, as well as reasonable solutions and procedures to follow when they cannot be resolved. If possible, you should keep a log of the occasions when colleagues requested your assistance and the action you took. This log should be kept over a period of time, eg one month, and include requests from colleagues and superiors, plus the action you have taken.

Claiming credit

Once you have completed your final assessment, you will need to write in your record book or folder *how, when, where* and *what* you have done to prove that you are competent.

The following is an example of how one trainee completed this claim.

8.2.a During my work and time at the training centre I made sure that when colleagues asked me to assist I helped them politely and willingly.

8.2.b When I was too busy to help I told my colleagues why I was unable to help and estimated when I would be free to assist. I made sure I was polite and courteous at all times.

8.2.c If difficulties or disagreements occurred, I discussed them with my colleague and reached an understanding which both of us accepted.

8.2.d If any difficulties or disagreements could not be settled, I would discuss these with my tutor, supervisor or department manager.

UNIT 9
Health and safety

Element 9.1
OPERATE SAFELY IN THE WORKPLACE

There are legal health and safety requirements that have to be followed in both the office and in other working areas. Health and safety laws cover lighting, heating, space, cleanliness, ventilation, and so on, to ensure that people work in an environment that is safe and comfortable. As an employee, you will benefit from working in such an environment. As an employer, the benefit is that working time lost through poor working conditions, illness or accident is reduced.

► *What types of office are there?*

There are many types of office, varying according to the work carried out in them. In terms of health and safety, it is important to recognise different office layouts. The two main styles of layout are 'open plan' and 'closed'.

1 An open plan office. A large space is furnished and divided up into different sections (possibly departments), using plants, filing cabinets and acoustic screens (used to prevent noise travelling). Staff using the same information and equipment can be grouped together, but central services used by all staff, such as photocopying, can be placed in a central position for all staff to use.

Some of the advantages of this layout are:

- easier supervision of staff
- better communication
- cheaper to run
- staff have closer contact

Fig 9.1 Part of an open plan office

Disadvantages would include:

- more noise
- less privacy
- less security
- more distraction

2 Closed offices are separate rooms accessed from a central corridor. This layout is more 'traditional' and resembles school corridors with classrooms leading off.

Some of the advantages of this layout are:

- better security
- more privacy
- less distraction
- less noise

Disadvantages would include:

- more space required
- more expensive to run
- more supervision required

In terms of health and safety, the open plan office is easier to operate because all staff are kept together in the same room. Fire-fighting

Fig 9.2 A first-aid box

equipment and first-aid boxes can be centralised and all staff can see who or what is affected by their actions. If there is an emergency, all staff would leave the office together, so there is less chance of someone being left behind. A central Health and Safety Officer can be elected to ensure that all laws are fully enforced.

■ DIY 9.1.1

It is vital that before you continue with this unit you are fully aware of your own organisation's emergency and fire procedures. Draw a plan on a piece of A4 paper of your office, or the most frequently-used area in your college or training centre. Use symbols to indicate the location of fire alarms, fire extinguishers, smoke/heat detectors, exits, fire doors, sprinklers, fire blankets, sand buckets, first-aid box and accident report documents. (Remember to show a key to these symbols, so they can be identified.) If any of these items is situated outside the area in your plan, find out where it is and write on a separate piece of paper the details of its location. Also include the name and location of the nearest trained first-aider.

▶ *What health and safety laws are there?*

There are two main laws in operation that affect you and your employer:

1 Health and Safety at Work Act 1974 (HASAWA)

This Act brings together many of the previous health and safety laws. The basic idea of the Act is that there should be a joint effort by employers and employees to provide a safe and healthy working environment.

The employer has to provide:

- safe equipment and systems of work
- safe working conditions and adequate arrangements and facilities for welfare
- safe use, storage, transport and handling of substances and articles
- a safe means of access to and from work

If an accident should occur the employer must investigate this fully. All staff should be fully informed, supervised and trained in accordance with their work role.

Employees are responsible for:

- taking care of their own safety
- the safety of other people affected by their actions
- co-operating with employers and any other persons involved in carrying out duties under this law

The HASAWA includes the Electricity at Work Regulations 1989 and The Reporting of Injuries, Diseases and Dangerous Occurrences Regulations 1985 (RIDDOR).

The Electricity at Work Regulations 1989. The purpose of the

Electricity at Work Regulations is to make sure precautions are taken against the risk of death or injury from electricity at work. The regulations include maintenance guidelines for all electrical equipment such as the office kettle, electric fan, word processor, and so on. All electrical equipment must be inspected and maintained on a regular basis – some organisations use stick-on labels saying if the equipment is authorised for use, the date of the last inspection and the date of the next inspection. Refer to the leaflet *Guidance for small businesses on electricity at work* produced by the Health and Safety Executive.

RIDDOR states that an accident book, form or record must be kept by anyone employing workers. If an accident does occur, the employer must keep a written account of what has happened, which is checked by the Local Authority Environmental Health Officer or an Inspector from the Health and Safety Executive. This information is used to identify accident trends and unsafe working practices. If an employer fails to provide an adequately safe and healthy place of work, they can be fined, closed down or even face imprisonment if they are a persistent offender. The Health and Safety Executive leaflets *Report that Accident* and *Reporting an injury or a dangerous occurrence* provide more details on these regulations.

■ DIY 9.1.2

Copy a page from an accident report book or ask your supervisor for an accident report form. Complete this form with the following details:

At 10.00 am today the accounts secretary, Zoe Thorner, who was celebrating her 18th birthday, tripped over a lead in the secretarial section of the Personnel Department. The lead was trailing across the floor from the word processor to the electric socket. Charlotte Vandy was with her at the time and was able to administer first aid to Zoe's twisted ankle. Zoe was taken home to 198 Tremlow Road, Wolverhampton, (or make up a local address) and is expected to have the next 4–5 days off work.

Who do you think caused this accident?

Write a memo to the Health and Safety Officer explaining how this accident occurred and what action you think should be taken to ensure that the same accident does not happen again.

Accident Report Form (To be completed by Line Manager)	
Accident Details:	Location:
	Department:
	Date: Time:
	Name & Address:
	Sex: Age:
Details of Injuries:	Occupation:
Signature ______________ (Line Manager)	Witnesses:
Distribution: Copy 1 to Human Resources Copy 2 to Facilities Manager Copy 3 to Health & Safety Representative Copy 4 to Facilities Manager Central Services Notification of Unsafe/Unhealthy Conditions form completed. YES/NO* (Only complete where necessary)	*Delete as applicable

Fig 9.3 An accident report form

2 The Office, Shops and Railway Premises Act 1963

This law states requirements that must be followed by the employer, such as:

- adequate floor space for each employee
- temperature above 16°C and a thermometer displayed
- adequate ventilation without draught
- adequate, separate toilets
- washing facilities with hot and cold water
- soap and clean drying facilities
- fresh drinking water
- facilities to hang and dry clothes
- isolation of noisy machinery
- safe and clear floors and stairways
- machinery or correct procedures to lift heavy weights
- chairs provided for employees who stand to do their work
- availability of trained first-aid staff
- adequately stocked first-aid boxes
- machine guards where necessary
- clear gangways and fire exits
- fire drills/assembly points brought to the notice of all staff
- adequate fire extinguishers in working order

The Information for Employees Regulations 1989 are provided to employers on a large poster that has to be displayed clearly in all offices. The poster informs employees of their rights and gives local information detailing the employees' local enforcing authority and the address of the local employment medical service.

■ DIY 9.1.3

Do you know where your *Information for Employees Regulations* poster is displayed? If not, find out. On a piece of A4 paper write the name and address of your local enforcing authority and the address of the local employment medical service.

▶ *What do you need to know about health and safety?*

The answer to this question is 'as much as possible', as it is your responsibility to look after yourself and others who may be affected by your actions. In the same way as an employer has a duty to protect employees, you as an employee have a duty to go about your work following safe working practices.

If you notice a potential hazard, it is vital that you tell your supervisor or the organisation's safety representative before someone has an accident. It is possible for you to contact the Health and Safety Executive, Local Authority Environmental Health Department or, perhaps, the local fire brigade if you feel your employer is putting people's health at risk.

In very general terms, all personnel in the workplace, college or training centre should know:

1 Names and location of trained first-aid staff
2 Location of accident report form, record or book
3 Location of first-aid box
4 What to do on discovering a fire
5 Where fire-fighting equipment is kept
6 How to select and operate equipment correctly

This information should be covered in the safety policy, rules and emergency procedures of the organisation. It should be explained during induction training and followed through daily routine by supervision, regular updating and adequate health and safety training.

■ DIY 9.1.4

Your office supervisor or tutor should have informed you of the procedures to be followed in the event of a fire or an emergency. There should be guidelines for you and other staff or trainees to follow – if you are unaware of these procedures, tell your supervisor or tutor immediately. Remember that if you work in ignorance of these procedures you not only risk your own life, but also the lives of others. Use two separate pieces of A4 paper to list (a) the procedure to be followed if there is a fire and (b) the procedure to follow if there is an emergency.

▶ *What first aid should be available?*

Under the Health and Safety (First Aid) Regulations 1981, organisations must have at least one trained first-aider for every 50 workers, students or trainees. However, in a more hazardous workplace such as a factory or quarry, more first-aiders would be required.

Qualified first-aid staff will have completed training and gained a certificate which is valid for three years. They are trained to administer treatment using the contents of an adequately-stocked first-aid box. This box should contain:

- individually-wrapped sterile dressings of assorted sizes
- sterile eye-pads with attachment
- individually-wrapped triangular bandages
- safety pins
- medium, large and extra large size sterile individually-wrapped, unmedicated wound dressings
- cleaning tissues, cotton wool, antiseptic, disposable gloves
- disposable wipes
- guidance notes on Health and Safety Regulations
- reorder forms
- list of contents

First-aid boxes should only contain the items that a first-aider has been trained to use. They should not contain medication of any kind. The Health and Safety Executive leaflet *First aid in your work place* will give you more information.

Note: If you have a First Aid Certificate place a copy in your work folder – this will give you credit towards the assessment for this unit.

▶ *What fire-fighting equipment is available?*

Equipment available will depend upon the type of fire risk that may occur. For example, it would be pointless to provide extinguishers for oil fires if the organisation never used oil! You may find sand buckets, fire blankets, water hoses and different coloured fire extinguishers in the building, but do you know what type of fire each should be used for? The following information will help you.

FIRE EXTINGUISHERS		
Colour	**Contents**	**Use for fires**
GREEN	Halon, BCF	Paper, wood, fabric, liquids, fat, paint, spirits, oils, gases (such as oxygen, butane and propane), and electrical fires.
CHROME	Gas	As above.
CREAM	Foam	As above, but not electrical fires.
BLACK	CO2	Liquids, fat, paint, spirits, oil, gases and electrical fires.
BLUE	Powder	Metals, such as magnesium, on fire.
RED	Water	Paper, wood and fabric fires.

Fig 9.4 Chart of use of fire extinguishers

Fire extinguishers will also have clear labels stating their contents and the type of fire for which they are suitable. The basic principle of using an extinguisher is to smother the fire – in other words, to cut off the oxygen supply at the base of the fire so it will die. Directions of use for each extinguisher should be shown on the label.

Fire blankets and sand buckets may also be available, these too are used to smother the fire and should be used in accordance with instructions.

Fire alarms are provided by most organisations. These should be activated immediately if you discover a fire. There may also be smoke-sensitive/heat-sensitive alarms which will activate automatically if there is smoke in the air or if the temperature rises above a certain level. Sprinklers may also be used, which release jets of water if they detect smoke.

Organisations, in an attempt to prevent fire, often implement a no-smoking policy in their buildings. A cigarette end dropped into a wastepaper basket may be all that is needed to start a fire! However, areas such as the rest room or coffee lounge are often set aside for smokers, in an attempt to prevent them going somewhere 'sneaky' for a cigarette! If you do smoke, make sure you are doing this in an authorised area, and not sneaking off to the toilets where smoking is not officially allowed.

▶ *When is a door not a door?*

You probably know the answer to: 'When is a door not a door?'. The answer is 'When it's ajar'! Indeed, when a door is left open, it might as well not be there! You may find that there are doors in your organisation marked with the words 'fire door – do not leave open'. These doors are there for a purpose, to hold back fire and give people more time to evacuate the building, so if they are left open they cannot do this.

It is important that you do not confuse these doors with 'fire exits'. A fire exit may be left open (with permission), perhaps to let air into the office, as its purpose is to allow people to escape in the event of fire. It is important that you understand the difference between these two types of door and never prop open a door that is marked as a fire door.

■ DIY 9.1.5

You should now be aware of some of the possible risks in an office. Copy out the list in Fig 9.5.(You may type this if you wish and present it to others as a useful health and safety questionnaire.) In order to ensure that your own work area is kept free from hazards, complete the list for your own work area.

▶ *What are the possible hazards?*

These are many and varied, depending on the environment and type of work being carried out. An office may not be the most likely place to find hazards dangerous to health, but accidents do still happen if safe

SAFE AND TIDY CHECKLIST			
Question	Answer		
	Yes	No	Comments
FILING CABINETS 1 Are drawers left open? 2 Can more than one drawer be opened at once? 3 Are drawers overcrowded?			
TELEPHONE 1 Is it easy to reach? 2 Are wires kept out of the way? 3 Is the mouthpiece clean?			
COMPUTER 1 Is brightness correct? 2 Are screen and keyboard positioned correctly? 3 Do you have enough light without glare?			
DESK 1 Is it tidy? 2 Is it an obstruction? 3 Is it the right height? 4 Is all equipment stored safely?			
CHAIR 1 Is it comfortable? 2 Does it support your back? 3 Do you leave it in gangways?			

Fig 9.5 Safe and tidy checklist

working practices are not followed.

Think of the accidents that may occur if you work in an office that has:

- slippery or poorly maintained floors
- staircases and fire exits used as storage space

- fire doors left open
- frayed carpets, with loose threads or holes
- trailing electric leads
- obstacles in gangways
- faulty electrical equipment
- no training on how to lift heavy objects
- no steps to reach high shelving
- no safety guards on machines

There are many more hazards in an office. Examples are: drawers left open; cabinets placed in front of fire extinguishers; open scissors or sharp objects left on table tops; chairs left in gangways; and overloaded electric sockets. Are you guilty of throwing items such as pens, sticky tape and correction fluid across the room to a colleague? Many people do this and it is only after an accident has occurred that they think twice before doing it again.

It is very important that we are all able to recognise potential hazards and avoid actions that may cause accidents. You should be aware of

Fig 9.6 Some safety hazards in the office

how to behave in an office and not put the safety of yourself or your colleagues at risk. Make sure that you know the procedures to follow and, if you are ever unsure of what to do, ask your supervisor.

▶ *How do you operate equipment safely?*

There is a very simple answer to this question! You should never operate any equipment or machinery in an office without first being shown how to operate it correctly by your supervisor. If a member of staff asks you to use any piece of equipment with which you are unfamiliar, simply apologise and explain that you have not used the equipment before and would like some help. It is far better to do this than possibly to injure yourself or put the equipment out of action!

Equipment such as folding machines, shredders, drills, laminators and even the office photocopier should have operating instructions or a manufacturer's manual giving you instructions on how to use the equipment safely and correctly. However, you should never be left alone with a piece of equipment until you have received a demonstration from your supervisor, who should then have observed you using the equipment correctly yourself.

■ DIY 9.1.6

Prepare your own instruction manual for the photocopier you use most often. This should not be copied directly from the manufacturer's manual, but should be written by you as if you were explaining to another person how to use the machine. Include drawings of the various indicators that light up to give you information, such as paper size and position, toner/paper refill required, and paper jam – explain what each indicator means. Also explain how the photocopier should be used safely: you will need to mention cleaning the glass top, closing the lid before copying and unplugging the machine at night.

It is also important to look after equipment. It may be your responsibility to clean or perhaps oil certain pieces of equipment, but check this with your supervisor first. Some organisations have a contract with an outside company who will take on the responsibility of maintaining, repairing and cleaning office equipment and machinery. It is important to remember that equipment which is maintained properly and treated with respect will last longer and is less likely to let you down.

You must be particularly careful with electrical equipment and always be on the look out for trailing or frayed electrical wires. Machines with blades, such as guillotines and shredders, should be used with respect and fingers should not be poked in to find a piece of missing paper. Machines that become hot with use should be handled with care, as for example the inside of a photocopier or laminating machine which will burn you if touched. Also be careful with equipment that uses toxic fluids such as spirit or ammonia, which are inflammable and give off fumes.

■ DIY 9.1.7

Do you know the correct way to pick up and move heavy items? If you do not want to suffer from a bad back in later life, now is a good time to find out! Carry out a search in your library and collect as much information as you can from leaflets and books. Prepare a sheet of A4 paper that can be used as an office poster, giving step-by-step instructions on how to pick up and move heavy items properly.

▶ *How will you be affected by new technology?*

In a modern office it is likely that you will use up-to-date equipment such as digital telephones, fax machines, computerised photocopiers and, of course, computers and word processors. New technology has the advantage of improving communication and increasing our output rates – in other words, producing more work in less time! The advantages of new technology far outweigh the disadvantages, although there has been concern over the effects on health through the use of VDU (visual display unit) screens.

The Health and Safety Executive has recommended a series of guidelines for ensuring that your health is not affected. The Health and Safety Executive leaflet *Working with VDUs* will give you more information, but the main recommendations are:

- availability of adjustable controls for screen brightness and contrast
- use of screen filters if required
- detachable keyboards that can be positioned to suit the individual
- slanted keyboards with matt colour surround to reduce glare
- adequate lighting that does not reflect off the screen
- ventilation and acceptable room temperature

- use of acoustic covers to reduce noise, or siting printers, etc, away from operators

There are no laws to say how long a person should be expected to work at a VDU, although a period of no longer than four hours without a break is often advised. Your ability to spend long periods of time in front of a VDU will depend on the work being carried out. Word processing may require rapid keyboarding, but, if you are able to touch type, this will result in little time being spent actually looking at the screen itself. However, composing text, spreadsheet and database input, and desk top publishing may require shorter work periods, because far greater concentration on the screen is necessary.

■ DIY 9.1.8

Below, you will find sentences that are incomplete. The sentences are relevant to work already covered. Copy out these sentences and fill in the missing word(s), which you can select from the following lists:

1 *acoustic plan plants open photocopying closed*
2 *employees health joint safety work at and*
3 *trends practices accident unsafe book*
4 *representative supervisor safety*
5 *first-aid medication three training certificate*
6 *fire shut open evacuate door*

1 There are two main types of office layout: ____ ____ and ______. In an open-plan office _________ screens and ______ are often used as dividers. Central services, such as _____________, can be placed in a central position for all staff to use.

2 There are two main health and safety laws in operation: ______ ___ ______ __ ____ Act 1974 and the Office, Shops and Railway Premises Act 1963. The basic idea of the HASAWA is that there should be a _____ effort by employers and __________ to provide a safe and healthy working environment.

3 The HASAWA includes The Reporting of Injuries, Diseases and Dangerous Occurrences Regulations 1985. RIDDOR states that an _________ ____ must be kept by anyone employing workers. The information held in this report is used to identify accident ______ and ______ working __________.

4 If you notice a potential hazard, you must tell the __________ or the organisation's ______ ______________ before someone has an accident.

5 Qualified first-aid staff will have completed ________ and gained a ___________ to prove they are competent. This certificate is valid for _____ years and trains staff to administer treatment using a _____-___ box. This box should not contain __________ of any kind.

6 A fire exit may be left ____ (with permission), but a ____ ____ should always be kept ____ as its purpose is to hold back fire and give people more time to ________ the building.

Completing Unit 9

To complete this unit on operating safely in the workplace, you will need to put all DIY tasks into your work folder and carry out a final assessment. This assessment can be carried out by your supervisor or tutor using ongoing observation over a period of time. It should prove that you keep your own work area free from hazards, use equipment according to instructions, recognise, rectify and/or report potential hazards, report promptly and record accidents accurately.

Claiming credit

Once you have completed your final assessment, you will need to write in your record book or folder *how, when, where* and *what* you have done to prove that you are competent.

The following is an example of how one trainee completed this claim:

9.1.a While on work placement at Coopers and Co, from 5.5.9– to 23.5.9–, I worked in the Personnel Department, where I kept my desk tidy and stored equipment safely.

9.1.b My supervisor showed me how to use the photocopier and franking machine properly. I was also given operating instructions which I followed at all times.

9.1.c I did not recognise/rectify hazards at Cooper and Co, but did complete a college assignment where I had to make recommendations for the prevention of accidents (see work folder).

9.1.d In a college assignment I had to complete an accident report form accurately according to college policy (see work folder).

Note: You will find that there are also health and safety elements in other units. You must complete these according to the content of the unit to prove that you understand the requirements of health and safety when carrying out different tasks. For example, Unit 7, Reprographics, Element 7.1.h, will require you to explain how you used reprographic equipment safely. You will need to say something like: I always put the lid down when photocopying and I switched the machine off at night. If there was a paper jam or the machine needed more paper, I corrected this, but called my supervisor if anything else went wrong.

INDEX